57

SHRM
Q&A
SERIES

Frequently Asked Questions About Workplace Safety and Security

57

SHRM
Q&A
SERIES

Frequently Asked Questions About Workplace Safety and Security

with Answers from

SHRM's Knowledge Advisors

Edited by Margaret Fiester, SPHR-CA

Society for Human Resource Management
Alexandria, Virginia I www.shrm.org

Strategic Human Resource Management India
Mumbai, India I www.shrmindia.org

Society for Human Resource Management
Haidian District Beijing, China I www.shrm.org/cn

Founded in 1948, the Society for Human Resource Management (SHRM) is the world's largest HR membership organization devoted to human resource management. Representing more than 275,000 members in over 160 countries, the Society is the leading provider of resources to serve the needs of HR professionals and advance the professional practice of human resource management. SHRM has more than 575 affiliated chapters within the United States and subsidiary offices in China, India and United Arab Emirates. Visit us at shrm.org.

Cover Design: Katrina Lambird

Interior Design: Shirley E.M. Raybuck

Library of Congress Cataloging-in-Publication Data

53 frequently asked questions about workplace safety and security : with answers from SHRM's knowledge advisors / edited by Margaret Fiester, SPHR-CA.

pages cm

Includes bibliographical references and index.

ISBN 978-1-58644-361-0

1. Work environment--Safety measures. 2. Industrial safety. 3. Industrial hygiene. I. Fiester, Margaret. II. Society for Human Resource Management (U.S.) III. Title: Fifty-three frequently asked questions about workplace safety and security.

HD7261.A13 2014

658.3'82--dc23

2014003963

14-0066

Contents

Introduction

This book contains frequently asked questions and answers gathered over the years by the Society for Human Resource Management's HR Knowledge Advisors in response to members' questions on various workplace health, safety, and security related topics. The book provides short answers to these questions for the benefit of HR generalists or individuals new to the HR function, who may not be familiar with the laws, regulations, and best practices relative to mitigating the risks associated with safety and security.

Acknowledgments

SHRM's Knowledge Center is a free service to SHRM members. SHRM's Knowledge Advisors are certified, highly experienced HR generalists who provide information resources and practical advice in response to SHRM members' HR-related questions. Knowledge Advisors develop HR-related content, including Q&As, for SHRM's website. This book is dedicated to the Knowledge Advisors.

Chapter 1

Accidents and Injuries

Q: Are employers required to have a first aid kit, and, if so, what items must it include?

The General Duty Clause of the Occupational Safety and Health Administration (OSHA) requires all employers to provide employees with a safe and healthy workplace that is reasonably free of occupational hazards.[1] However, it is unrealistic to expect accidents not to happen. Therefore, employers are required to provide medical and first aid personnel and supplies commensurate with the hazards of the workplace. According to OSHA, the details of a workplace medical and first aid program are dependent on the circumstances of each workplace and employer.

Employers should keep in mind that medical and first aid services are addressed in specific standards for general industry, shipyard employment, marine terminals, longshoring, and the construction industry. The standards for general industry may be found in 29 C.F.R., Section 1910.151.[2] The other standards may be found by searching for the specific industry on the OSHA website.[3]

Employers may also find the following standard interpretations to be helpful. These interpretations explain the requirements and their applicability to particular circumstances.

- Interpretation of the first aid standard.[4]
- OSHA first aid standard. Discusses frequency of training.[5]
- Standard for medical services and first aid. With regard

to the specific contents of first aid kits, workplaces vary widely in their degree of hazards, location, size, amount of staff training, and availability of professional medical services. With the exception of the Logging Operations Standard, OSHA standards do not require specific first aid kit contents.[6]

Employers may find it helpful to refer to a list of basic first aid supplies, available in the American National Standards Institute (ANSI) Standard, Z308.1, Minimum Requirements for Workplace First Aid Kits and Supplies (see Table 1.1). First aid kits in compliance with this standard will provide a basic range of products to deal with most types of injuries encountered in the workplace and may be adequate for a small worksite. Employers should evaluate their own workplaces to determine whether additional supplies or kits are needed based on the size and specific hazards of their workplaces.

Table 1.1	Minimum Requirements for Workplace First Aid Kits and Supplies Basic Kit: Minimum Contents	
Item	Minimum Quantity
Absorbent compress, 32 sq. in. (206 sq. cm.) with no side smaller than 4 in. (10 cm.)	1
Adhesive bandages, 1 in. x 3 in. (2.5 cm. x 7.5 cm.)	16
Adhesive tape, 3/8 in. x 2.5 yd. (2.3 m.)	1
Antibiotic treatment, 0.14 oz. (0.5 g.)	6
Antiseptic, 0.14 fl. oz. (0.5 g.) application 2	10
Burn treatment, 1/32 oz. (0.9 g.) application 3	6
First-aid guide	1
Medical exam gloves	2 pair
Sterile pads, 3 in. x 3 in. (7.5 x 7.5 cm.)	4
Triangular bandage, 40 in. x 40 in. x 56 in. (101 cm. x 101 cm. x 142 cm.)	1

In a similar fashion, employers that have unique or changing first aid needs in their workplace may need to enhance their first aid kits. Employers can refer to the OSHA 300 log, OSHA 301 log, or other reports to identify these unique problems. OSHA recommends consulting with the local fire/rescue department, appropriate medical professionals, or the local emergency room. By assessing the specific needs of their workplace, employers can ensure that reasonably anticipated supplies are available. OSHA also recommends that employers periodically assess specific needs of their worksite and augment the first aid kit appropriately.

Q: I have been tasked with lowering accident rates, but I have no budget to train employees. What should I do?

Proper training is essential to maintaining a safe workplace. However, in this era of ever-tightening budgets, training is often a line item that is either slashed drastically or left off the budget altogether. Some experts argue that reduced accident rates, lost time at work, and workers' compensation claims far outweigh the investment an employer can make in safety training. But what do you do if your organization does not have the funds to make that investment? Below are some ideas to get you started.

- Send just one employee to training. Select one employee to attend the formal training with the understanding that when the employee returns, he or she must train the rest of his or her colleagues on what was covered in the training. For this strategy to be successful, the organization needs to select an employee who will be attentive and participative during the training. It also helps to select an employee who already has some familiarity with the topic being covered.

- Use more experienced employees. Safety training is a repetitive topic, and some more experienced employees may have already attended this training in the past. These employees can provide insight for newer employees. More experienced employees can also be used for their legacy knowledge in working on different types of equipment or determining which processes are the best. Human resources can gather a team of these employees and use their expertise to create customized training for the workplace.

- Use community resources. Local government agencies and nonprofits such as your local health department or the American Red Cross usually provide training at little cost compared with their private, for-profit counterparts. These resources would be useful for mandated trainings such as first aid and CPR.
- Explore web-based options. Online training can often be far less expensive than sending an employee to a seminar. For safety training, this option can be useful for compliance trainings and other general topic items.
- Contact OSHA. OSHA has an online training site dedicated to worker safety training.[7] The site contains not only free training materials and resources, but also information on numerous training grants available to employers.
- Contact your workers' compensation carrier. Many private and state-run workers' compensation carriers have in-house safety experts who are often available to conduct training at significantly reduced fees.

Workplace safety is closely tied to the organizational culture supported by the leadership and management of the entire organization. To enhance the safety program, organizations may want to include a "lessons learned" or best-practice program, in addition to their regular training. And though building a world-class workplace safety program takes time, dedication, and commitment, it need not break the budget.

Q: What are the recommended steps in an accident investigation?

The National Safety Council defines an accident as an "unplanned, undesired event, not necessarily resulting in injury, but damaging to property and/or interrupting the activity in process." The council defines an incident as "an undesired event that may cause personal harm or other damage."[8]

Although OSHA does not have specific standards for accident investigation, as a best practice, all accidents and incidents should be investigated, regardless of severity, including near-miss incidents in which no damage or harm resulted.

The following steps should be taken when conducting an accident investigation.

- Determine what happened.
- Describe the incident that took place—in other words, what prompted the investigation?
- Determine why the incident occurred.
- Establish the facts surrounding the occurrence. This is the heart of the investigation—the investigator must determine who, what, when, where, and why.
- Find out if a previous action been taken to correct the problem. If so, what was it? Why did it fail this time?
- Learn what should be done going forward to correct the problem.
- Identify any new methods that should be used to correct the problem. Is there a way to eliminate the cause(s) of the incident?

The following questions should be asked when performing an investigation:

1. What was the employee doing at the time of the accident?
2. Was the employee qualified to perform this operation?

3. Were company procedures being followed?
4. Is the job or process new?
5. Were proper tools or equipment being used?
6. Was the proper supervision being provided?
7. Had the employee received training on this operation prior to the accident?
8. Where was the location of the accident?
9. What was the physical condition of the area when the accident occurred? For example, what was the temperature of the area? If outside, was the ground wet or muddy? Was there debris in the way, or was the area clear?
10. What were witnesses doing at the time of the accident?
11. What immediate or temporary action could have prevented the accident or minimized its effect?
12. What long-term or permanent action could have prevented the accident or minimized its effect?
13. Had corrective action been recommended in the past but not adopted?

Q: What steps should an employer take when an employee sustains a work injury and is bleeding?

Any work injury is cause for concern, but when blood is present, employers need to act quickly and responsibly to protect the injured employee and others, as well as to take steps to reduce their liability. When an accident occurs and an employee is bleeding, an employer should take the steps outlined below:

- Determine if emergency medical assistance is needed. Look for signs such as bleeding that cannot be stopped, difficulty breathing, unresponsiveness, intense pain, or other signs of shock. Call 911 immediately; have an employee trained in safety and emergency response procedures meet the ambulance at the main door and direct EMTs to the injured employee. If the incident is not an emergency, remove the employee from the area when he or she is stable and no longer bleeding, apply first aid, and determine if further medical treatment should be sought.

• Consider OSHA obligations as they relate to exposure to blood in the workplace. The scope of OSHA's bloodborne pathogens rule is quite broad. If employees have a "reasonably anticipated" exposure to bloodborne pathogens, then they are covered by the standard. Therefore, assume that anyone rendering first aid would be covered. Please see OSHA's "Most Frequently Asked Questions Concerning the Bloodborne Pathogens Standard" for additional information.[9]

According to the standard, all blood spills should be immediately contained and cleaned up by staff qualified to work with potentially concentrated infectious materials, employing universal precautions such as donning gloves, eye protection, and masks (see SHRM's bloodborne pathogens sample policy for guidance[10]). Warn others within the immediate area, and block off the area of the spill. A trained employee should then clean all equipment and working surfaces according to OSHA standards.[11] Employers should have at least two to three individuals trained in handling such situations. In nonmedical environments, employers usually provide training to individuals in areas with greater risk of workplace injuries (where heavy machinery or other heavy equipment is used). In a regular office setting, some employers train individuals in their building facilities group, whereas others may train at least one individual in each of their larger departments or divisions.

• Determine if other employees were exposed to the blood. Often co-workers working nearby or those who provide immediate aid to the injured employee will have come in contact with the blood. Per OSHA standards, ensure these employees wash all affected skin with soap and water, and keep a list of all exposed employees and their job classifications.

When the immediacy of the situation has subsided, employers should conduct an accident investigation to determine what occurred, report the information to their workers' compensation carrier, and decide what actions may be necessary to avoid future accidents.[12]

If the injury or accident involves cuts from sharp objects that are contaminated with another person's blood or other potentially infectious material, the injury must be reported on the OSHA 300 log. Employers will also need to arrange for a medical evaluation and follow-up for the employee. OSHA's "Bloodborne Pathogen Exposure Incident" fact sheet provides additional guidance.[13]

Chapter 2
Business Continuity and Recovery

Q: What is the best way to plan for disasters that may affect a company?

Disasters, whether natural or manmade, can have a severe impact on business operations. Therefore, employers must be prepared to keep their employees safe and minimize disruptions to operations.

A systematic plan for approaching emergencies usually involves an understanding of the universe of hazards that may occur, followed by an assessment of the probabilities of these disasters occurring. Plans should be focused on the elements that have the highest degree of probability.

An employer's disaster preparedness plan should consider the following steps:

- Establish evacuation procedures, and communicate them to every employee; routinely conduct evacuation drills (as well as fire drills).
- Maintain accurate emergency contact information to reach employees and next of kin.
- Establish and publicize mechanisms (for example, intranet, phone, recorded announcement) through which the employer may inform its employees of any pertinent developments.
- Reassess the means and manner in which critical information is stored, both physically and electronically, to prevent irreparable physical damage from crippling the company's operations.

- Review existing property, casualty, business interruption, life, and other insurance policies, and modify such coverage where necessary or prudent.

When planning, the magnitude of the disaster must be considered. Different plans, and therefore differing resources, will be available should the disaster be local, regional, national, or even global.

Employers should develop a plan for identifying potential alternative worksite arrangements and staffing options, as well as the technology structures required to support business operations if worksites are inaccessible.

Employers are likely to have three employee groups based on the nature and magnitude of the emergency: employees who are severely affected (including those who have lost family members or homes, or those who are personally affected by severe illness); employees who have experienced situations such as energy or transportation losses as a result of the disaster; and employees who are not directly affected. Employers must develop policies for each employee group with consideration for their needs and issues.

HR professionals must evaluate the impact of a disaster or emergency on the organization's government reporting requirements. Emergency planning should take into consideration requirements with regard to the Occupational Safety and Health Administration (OSHA), COBRA, state laws requiring delivery of paychecks, Worker Adjustment and Retraining Notification (WARN) Act notifications, and I-9 reporting requirements, among many others.

All plans should be reviewed and updated periodically to determine that organizational changes have been taken into consideration (for example, new facilities, additional departments, changed organizational structure). Further, the plans should also include the latest emergency information, such as updates on epidemics and workplace considerations, or changes in protocols for responding to global disasters. In addition, plan resources and contact information should be periodically checked to ensure accuracy

Q: What steps should a company take to remain open during inclement weather?

Many employers operate 24 hours a day, 365 days a year. Whether it is a local hospital that must stay open at all costs or a manufacturing plant that cannot afford to shut down its machines, nonstop operations are the status quo for many businesses. For employers that operate in this type of business environment, it is vitally important for both the continuation of the business and the safety of employees to have a plan in place to address how operations will continue in the event a storm hits.

The key is to develop an inclement weather plan, communicate the plan, and practice the plan before the storm hits.[1] For some businesses, an inclement weather plan is part of a business continuity plan, which details how operations would continue in a variety of scenarios.[2] The focus of the plan should be striking a balance between keeping employees safe and keeping the business running.

The plan should define which employees are essential to the running of the business and must continue to work in the event of a weather emergency. Once the key employees are identified, the next step is to determine the best method for ensuring that they make it safely to the worksite. Common methods include setting up carpools, renting nearby hotel rooms for employees, and providing cots onsite so that employees can sleep.

The next step is to identify the employees who must work but do not necessarily need to be on the premises. Identifying these employees will likely require advance planning—for example, asking employees to take work equipment such as phones or computers home, so that they can telecommute more easily.

For all other nonessential employees, a common system employers use is a liberal leave policy. A liberal leave policy allows employees the choice to use paid leave instead of coming to work when inclement weather strikes.[3] Employees are given the freedom to use unapproved leave; this allows them to take the day off should they feel it is too dangerous to get to work or if they are simply unable to do so.

Employers without a plan in place should use their best judgment and ensure the safety of their employees. Not having a plan will likely result in lower production during the storm and increased unplanned expenses to transport employees to work safely.

Chapter 3
Communicable Disease

Q: **Can employers require employees to be vaccinated for communicable diseases, and, if so, must they pay for it?**

Employers can offer flu and other communicable disease vaccinations to employees *on a voluntary basis* through an employee health program and can strongly urge them to be vaccinated. One good method to encourage employees is to offer vaccinations during work time and at no cost to the employee.

In pandemic situations, federal or state emergency regulations may mandate vaccinations for certain personnel (e.g., public safety or health care employees). Some state laws require that employment testing, medical exams, and business expenses be paid for or reimbursed by the employer. Therefore, if your organization is mandated to vaccinate workers, you are probably required to cover all related costs as well.

Unless your organization falls under a federal or state regulation mandate, it is not recommended that employers make vaccinations a requirement of continued employment. First, it may be difficult and expensive to obtain enough vaccines for your entire workforce in time. Second, employees may have allergic reactions to vaccinations. Third, there may be other private medical reasons workers should not be vaccinated, creating concerns with potential Americans with Disabilities Act (ADA) violations.[1] Fourth, some employees may believe vaccines are against their religious beliefs, creating concern about violations of Title VII of the Civil Rights Act of 1964. Thus, the better course of action for employers is to conclude that a vaccination is a medical decision best left up to the employee and his or her doctor.

Employers should establish policies and procedures to help reduce the spread of germs during a pandemic. These include policies to encourage employees who feel ill or who may have been exposed to a communicable disease to remain home, policies allowing employees to telecommute when possible, or procedures to help employees reduce face-to-face contact (for example, conduct conference calls rather than traditional meetings). In addition, employers should post information on proper coughing/sneezing and hand-washing practices, take extra care in cleaning the work environment, and make tissues and hand sanitizers readily available throughout the workplace.

Q: Can a company require employees returning from an infected pandemic area to take leave or work from home until the incubation period for communicable disease is over?

There are no laws that would prohibit an employer from requiring an employee to remain away from the worksite as a precaution. Under the General Duty Clause of the Occupational Safety and Health Administration (OSHA), employers have an obligation to protect their workforce from known hazards, and taking precautions to contain the spread of communicable diseases could fall under that requirement.[2] Care should be taken, however, not to discriminate unlawfully against an employee with an actual or assumed medical condition—or you may run afoul of the ADA.[3]

In addition, there are pay issues to consider. The Fair Labor Standards Act requires that exempt employees be paid their full week's salary when they perform any work in a week.[4] If there are absences occasioned by the employer during such a week, the exempt employee must still be paid his or her full week's salary. Therefore, you may require the use of accrued paid time off (PTO) if your policy allows for it but an exempt employee must be fully paid even if he or she has no PTO available. This means that you will need to either advance leave or opt to pay for this time as regular pay.

Although employers do not have to pay exempt employees who perform no work in an entire workweek and are only required to pay nonexempt employees for actual hours worked, there are still employee morale and possible discrimination issues to be concerned with. An employee traveling at the company's request may feel that he or she is being treated unfairly if upon return the individual must use accrued paid leave simply for doing his or her job. Others traveling for personal reasons may feel they have been singled out due to their national origin (those visiting family in heavily infected areas, for example), which could lead to discrimination claims. Therefore, before implementing the policy, an employer is wise to review recommendations and guidance from sources such as the Centers for Disease Control and Prevention (CDC),[5] OSHA,[6] and the World Health Organization,[7] and speak with an attorney to ensure safety and prevent unlawful discriminatory factors from being used to administer the policy. Consider company culture and fairness to employees when requiring them to stay away from the worksite. Before docking PTO banks or pay, try to work out a way for employees to work from home or, if not symptomatic, return to the office with limited access to others and strict guidance on precautions to take, such as increased hand washing and social distancing of at least six feet. If this is not possible, consider paying regular wages as a temporary emergency measure for a specified time frame or offering unpaid leave instead of making the employee use accrued paid leave. In all instances, make sure you are communicating openly and often with all employees on measures being taken and precautions they can take to reduce the potential spread of disease.

Q: Employees are worried about contracting a communicable disease such as influenza from other employees. What should a company do to reassure them?
Dealing with illness in the workplace can be challenging at any time, but it is especially challenging during flu season. To help reassure employees, employers should provide information on the company's efforts to keep employees healthy. Below are suggestions on what to include in the communication.

- Inform employees that the company will take any steps necessary to ensure a safe and healthy work environment. If the situation changes, employees will be updated on those changes and how they may be affected.
- Include information on the disease, including any known symptoms and how to protect against getting the disease— in the case of influenza, washing hands frequently, covering one's mouth when coughing or sneezing, avoiding contact with sick individuals, and practicing proper hygiene.
- Make tissues and hand sanitizers available to employees. Educate employees on proper ways of washing hands and what to do if flu-like symptoms develop. Communication about these precautions should occur frequently, and employers should hang posters in bathrooms and eating areas on the proper way to stop the spread of germs. Depending on the industry and employees' proximity to others, an employer may also wish to provide respirators or masks to employees in the workplace to further hinder the spread of airborne germs.
- Advise employees of any changes to policies—for example, relaxing attendance policies to encourage sick employees to stay at home or reminding employees of applicable telecommuting policies.
- Notify employees of any discontinued travel, if applicable.

• Ask employees to remain calm and to come to human resources with any concerns.

Communication regarding this situation will help maintain order in the workplace and dissuade any potential fears employees may have.

Q: We have learned that an employee had a tuberculosis test. What should we do?

The fact that an employee had a tuberculosis (TB) test should not ordinarily be a concern. The test was possibly required for a second job, admission to a college, or participation in a volunteer program.

However, upon learning that an employee has tested positive for TB, an employer should take action. TB is a highly infectious disease. Some individuals may test positive, carry the infection, and not be contagious many years before developing the disease, whereas others who test positive may have already developed symptoms.

If the employee tests positive, it is not necessary to know how far the employee is in the progression of the disease. The focus should be on other employees and efforts to reduce the possibility of the disease spreading.

After learning that an employee has tested positive, the employer should contact the local health department to assist in determining possible risk to other employees and customers and to comply with any state requirements in reporting infectious diseases. The employee can also be required to provide a return-to-work release from a health care provider. If a release is not provided, it is best to follow company leave policies and require the release before allowing the employee to return to work.

Other employees should be notified, without identifying the actual employee who tested positive, that a case of TB has been reported in the workplace. The employer can provide the link to the CDC website on TB[8] and encourage employees to contact their physician if they begin to show signs or symptoms of TB.[9]

Employers should contact their state health department for more information on TB or other communicable diseases.[10]

Q: What is an employer's responsibility when dealing with communicable disease in the workplace?

An employer's responsibility is to provide a healthy, safe working environment for all its employees, even if there are no current standards governing the work area or the industry. The General Duty Clause of the Occupational Safety and Health (OSH) Act, Section 5(a)(1), addresses this issue.[11] It entitles an employee to "a place of employment which is free from recognized hazards that cause or are likely to cause death or serious physical harm."

Therefore, when an employer has an employee with a communicable disease, it should make every effort to reduce the possibility of the disease spreading. A good way to accomplish this is by training and educating the workforce on ways to reduce the spread of communicable disease. The CDC has information on communicable diseases—types, symptoms, and precautions—as well as resources related to training.[12] OSHA has prepared guidelines that, although specific to influenza outbreaks in the workplace, contain information and tips for dealing with communicable diseases at work.[13]

The employer may also implement a policy that requires an employee to inform the employer when the employee poses a direct threat to the safety of other employees. Employers must keep employees' health information confidential and must also ensure that any policy is in compliance with the ADA.[14] For employers in the restaurant and food service industry, the U.S. Equal Employment Opportunity Commission has published guidelines for dealing with employees with communicable diseases.[15]

In cases of bloodborne pathogen exposure, primarily found in health care settings, OSHA states that employers must offer any employees that have been exposed free medical evaluation and treatment by a licensed health care provider.[16] The provider will tell them what to do to prevent further spread of the disease and provide a written report to the employer indicating the results of the testing. The actual medical records are confidential and not made available to the employer. The records must be maintained for the duration of the employee's tenure plus an additional 30 years, in accordance with OSHA standards.

An infected employee also has privacy rights. Employers should take great care to ensure that the employee's privacy is protected.

Q: What protection can employers offer high-risk employees during flu season?

Employers should establish policies and procedures to protect all employees from communicable disease, although they should understand that the risks may be greater for certain workers. Employers must be open to discuss employee concerns and listen to their ideas and suggestions for ways to help them stay healthy. Employers can encourage employees who are at high risk to talk with their health care provider to determine what, if any, additional measures they should consider to keep themselves healthy and safe at work. Employers should strongly consider doctor's accommodation requests for high-risk workers.

Listed below are some of the suggested policies, practices, or protections that employers may consider as part of their preventive measures during an influenza pandemic, as discussed in OSHA's "Guidance on Preparing Workplaces for an Influenza Pandemic."[17]

- Establish policies to encourage employees who feel ill to stay home.
- Encourage employees, especially high-risk employees, to telework.

- Allow employees to work flexible work schedules to limit the number of workers in the same work area or worksite.
- Reduce face-to-face contact (for example, conduct conference calls rather than traditional meetings).
- Post reminders on proper hand-washing and coughing/sneezing practices.
- Ensure work surfaces are cleaned regularly, especially in public areas and between shifts in shared areas.
- Make hand sanitizers and tissues available throughout the facility.
- Install clear plastic sneeze guards between employees and customers in face-to-face, customer-focused industries.
- Provide employees with appropriate personal protective equipment (PPE)— such as gloves, goggles, and respirators— as an accommodation for high-risk workers, or require it in more severe pandemic situations or areas.

Q: What steps should an employer take when an employee is exposed to lice at work?

As with many other conditions, understanding the nature of the issue is the first step, and this will help determine what to do next. Often, people associate lice with bad hygiene, but lice are a common problem, especially among children and adults in frequent contact with children. Lice are not dangerous and do not spread disease, but they are contagious and can be irritating. Their bites often cause an individual's scalp to become itchy and inflamed. Continued scratching may lead to skin irritation and even infection.

Lice are spread mainly through head-to-head contact, but sharing clothing, bed linens, and other items can spread them as well. In general, individuals most prone to catching lice are those who tend to have close physical contact with others.

If an employee has been exposed to lice at work, he or she

should be referred to a physician for treatment. The physician can recommend the best course of action, such as an over-the-counter (OTC) drug or a medicated shampoo, cream rinse, or lotion to kill the lice. Treating lice would not generally be covered under workers' compensation. You may choose to allow the employee personal leave time to seek treatment based on the company's leave policy. The employer should establish or refer to its policies for return-to-work criteria.

The CDC states that most health departments do not require employers to report head lice.[18] However, it may be prudent to send out a generic communication to employees via e-mail or handouts (if not all employees have access to e-mail), stating that an incident of head lice has been reported in the office or facility. Explain that the situation is unrelated to the cleanliness of the facility, and encourage employees to begin treatment with OTC medications if they experience symptoms and to contact their health care provider for further instructions.

Common areas should be thoroughly cleaned with disinfectant. Most notably, conference rooms with high-back chairs and designated nap areas should be disinfected. Of course, this should be done after the employees have left for the day or before they return in the morning.

Chapter 4
Drug and Alcohol Testing

Q: Can a company test an employee for substance abuse if there is no written substance abuse policy?

In most states, it generally is permissible for private-sector employers to test employees for substance abuse if the employer has a policy of doing so. Employers should have substance abuse policies reviewed by legal counsel to ensure compliance with state[1] and federal laws, including the Americans with Disabilities Act (ADA),[2] as well as with local ordinances and any applicable collective bargaining agreements.

Private-sector employers generally may select employees for testing randomly, may test before employment commences, and may test employees who have been involved in accidents. Employers may also train managers to watch for behaviors that indicate substance abuse.

A dilemma that employers face in taking action with employees who seem to exhibit signs of substance abuse is that many of the indicators of substance abuse might also be symptoms of disabilities such as strokes, neurological disorders, or mental illnesses that substantially limit major life activities. This makes it difficult for employers to select employees based on behavioral evidence without potentially singling out an employee based on disability.

A substance abuse testing policy should address which employees will be tested, the circumstances under which testing will take place, what substances will be tested for, and what the consequences will be for positive tests. The policy should be readily accessible to employees and written in clear, easily understood language.

The policy should explain how to obtain written consent from the employee on testing, as well as the consequences should an employee fail to grant written consent. Employers implementing a substance abuse testing policy should carefully select a qualified testing facility to conduct the tests, and should also set up procedures that ensure the confidentiality of test results.

Q: Must all companies follow the FCRA guidelines for drug tests?

It depends. Employers often use the term "background check" to describe a process that can include one or any combination of screening tools, including criminal records checks, credit reports, motor vehicle reports, reference checks, and drug-test results. The Fair Credit Reporting Act (FCRA) requires, among other things, that employers provide disclosure and obtain consent before securing a consumer report.

The Federal Trade Commission (FTC), which governs and enforces the FCRA, describes a consumer report as follows: "A consumer report contains information about your personal and credit characteristics, character, general reputation and lifestyle. To be covered by the FCRA, a report must be prepared by a consumer reporting agency (CRA)—a business that assembles such reports for other businesses."[3]

The FTC explains, "An intermediary that retains copies of tests performed by drug labs and regularly sells this information to third parties for a fee is a CRA whose reports of drug-test results are 'consumer reports' covered by the FCRA."[4]

In summary, some background check companies include drug-test results in their reporting services. *In this case*, it is likely that the drug test will be considered a consumer report. On the other hand, if an employer obtains the information directly from a drug-testing lab, it is less likely to be considered a "consumer report" and subject to the FCRA. The FTC offers specific guidance on drug tests as consumer reports.

Q: Many of our employees drive as part of their job. Are we required to test them for drugs?

Not necessarily. Just because an employee drives as part of his or her job does not mean that drug and alcohol testing is required. There may be practical reasons for implementing such a program, however. An employee who is in an accident while working can create financial liability as well as a negative public image for the company.

Employers receiving federal transportation funds are covered by the drug- and alcohol-testing regulations of the Department of Transportation (DOT). Also covered are contractors, operators, or sub-recipients that provide mass transportation or safety-sensitive services for employers that receive federal transportation funds.

Covered employees in safety-sensitive positions usually include commercial truckers, air carrier flight and support personnel, and railroad employees. These employees generally fall into the following categories:

- Commercial vehicle operators.
- Operators of nonrevenue service vehicles, if the job requires a commercial driver's license.
- Dispatchers and anyone who controls the dispatch or movement of revenue service vehicles or equipment used in revenue service.
- Maintenance personnel for revenue service vehicles (except cleaning crews).
- Security guards who carry firearms.

The DOT has developed a decision tree to assist employers in determining if they are covered by the DOT drug- and alcohol-testing requirements.[5]

Q: What are the requirements for drug testing commercial vehicle operators and employees who drive as part of the job?

The Omnibus Transportation Employee Testing Act of 1991 requires employers to set forth drug- and alcohol-testing requirements for employees who operate commercial vehicles.[6] The intent of the act is to increase transportation safety by mandating such testing for individuals in safety-sensitive positions.

The DOT publishes rules in accordance with the act for employers that must conduct the testing. Employers in the aviation, trucking, railroad, mass transit, pipeline, or maritime industries must implement required testing. DOT agencies, including the Federal Motor Carrier Safety Administration, the Federal Railroad Administration, the Federal Aviation Administration, the Federal Transit Administration, and the Pipeline and Hazardous Materials Safety Administration, as well as the U.S. Coast Guard, have industry-specific regulations for testing employees who perform safety-sensitive functions.

The act mandates pre-employment, reasonable suspicion, post-accident, random, and follow-up/return-to-duty drug and alcohol testing of employees in positions requiring a commercial driver's license and defined as safety-sensitive. The law prohibits commercial motor vehicle drivers from performing safety-sensitive functions after an alcohol test result indicating a 0.02 alcohol concentration or a positive drug-test result. The law also prohibits drivers from using alcohol or illegal drugs while on duty.

Employees covered by the act should be tested under the following circumstances:

- When assigned to a position requiring a commercial driver's license.
- On a random basis.
- After an accident that resulted in the employee being issued a citation for a moving vehicle violation or resulting in a fatality.
- For reasonable cause based on observed behavior or appearance.
- Before being allowed to return to a covered position after having tested positive for drug or alcohol abuse.

Although DOT regulations mandate the types of testing and the procedures to adhere to following a positive test result, the regulations do not address employment decisions such as hiring, firing, or leaves of absence. These decisions are up to the employer, in accordance with other applicable laws such as the ADA.

Employers are required by law to provide certain records of the employees' DOT drug- and alcohol-testing history to new employers on receipt of a signed written release. Employees or employers that violate the provisions of this law are subject to fines for each offense.

Q: What laws should companies be aware of when implementing a drug-testing program?

An employer establishing a drug and alcohol abuse policy must (a) take the ADA into account, (b) be aware of federal antidrug initiatives that affect contractors and employers in safety-sensitive industries, and (c) be familiar with applicable state law.

The ADA does not prevent an employer from taking steps to combat the use of drugs and alcohol in the workplace. It specifically provides for an employer to prohibit the use of drugs and alcohol and to prohibit employees from being under the influence of drugs or alcohol at work. An employer can discharge or deny employment to current users of illegal drugs without fear of being held liable for disability discrimination.

With regard to drug testing, the ADA sets limits on employment-related medical examinations. An employer is prohibited from requiring a job applicant to undergo medical testing before the employer has made a conditional offer of employment. However, a drug screen is not considered a medical test, and an employer can require applicants to take pre-employment drug tests. Alcohol testing, however, is considered a medical test and may not be performed prior to a conditional offer of employment.

An employer setting up a drug-testing program should be aware of federal antidrug initiatives.

- The Drug-Free Workplace Act covers federal government agencies, federal contractors with contracts or purchase orders totaling $25,000 or more, recipients of federal grants, and any individuals awarded federal contracts.[7] The act does not require alcohol or drug testing, but testing is authorized as a means to maintain a drug-free workplace.
- DOT drug-testing rules cover employers in the air, rail, trucking, and mass transit industries and employers with operations otherwise covered by DOT.[8] Those rules require the testing of employees in safety-sensitive positions for alcohol and illegal drug use.

Most states have laws that address workplace drug use and drug testing.[9] Some states require employers to put their testing program in writing. Other states prohibit disciplinary actions against employees who test positive without a second confirming test, or they require that testing be performed only in state-approved labs. Because states have their own approach to drug-testing issues, employers should carefully review the law in the states in which they operate before they adopt a drug-testing policy.

Q: Must drug-test results be kept confidential?

Generally, drug-test results, like all medical information about employees, should be kept confidential. Drug-test results should be filed in a confidential medical file separate from the general employee file.

The department that receives drug-test results should share results only on a need-to-know basis. For example, sharing drug-test results with front-line managers is often unnecessary beyond stating whether the results are pass or fail.

State drug-testing laws[10] or privacy laws may apply to drug-test results either specifically or generally as a matter of personal privacy. Also, the ADA[11] and the Health Insurance Portability and Accountability Act (HIPAA)[12] may apply to drug-test results depending on the facts involved. Employers should work with their attorneys to analyze relevance of these laws to drug-test results.

Drug-test results may also be critical in determining eligibility for state- and employer-sponsored benefits. Many laws recognize these situations. The DOT regulations on testing procedures permit the release of drug-test results for investigatory proceedings and other matters of necessity as described under 49 C.F.R. Section 40.323.[13] The U.S. Department of Labor (DOL) provides resources for employers on its website, including "Drug-Free Workplace Policy Builder, Section 7: Drug Testing."[14]

Examples of matters necessitating disclosure of test results include unemployment eligibility determination, workers' compensation claims, and disability benefits. Depending on the applicable laws, consented release may not even be required. However, a conservative approach, due to the various laws that may apply, would be to obtain written consent for release from the applicant or employee when possible. When not possible, employers should consult with an attorney before releasing information without signed authorization.

Chapter 5
Emergency Response

Q: Are there laws protecting an individual who offers care during an emergency situation?

On a federal level, "Good Samaritan" legislation has been enacted under the Cardiac Arrest Survival Act;[1] however, this legislation only covers the use of automated external defibrillators (AEDs) when assisting cardiac arrest victims.

Most states have enacted their own laws offering legal protection to individuals who voluntarily provide care during an emergency situation. Although these laws vary from state to state, they are typically referred to as Good Samaritan laws.

Good Samaritan laws were developed primarily as a means of encouraging people to provide assistance during emergency situations. They protect the rescuer from being sued and held financially responsible for a victim's illness or injury when the rescuer acts in a reasonable and prudent manner. Of course, individuals providing assistance during emergency situations should always exercise extremely good judgment as well as a reasonable level of skill not to exceed the scope of their own abilities or training.

Often, immunity under the statutes will be lost when the person providing care is found to have acted in a manner that was not reasonably prudent, to have been negligent or reckless, or to have abandoned the victim after initiating care. A reasonable and prudent person is considered to be one who:

- Moves a victim only if his or her life is endangered.

- Asks a conscious victim for permission prior to initiating care.
- Checks whether any life-threatening conditions exist before providing additional care.
- Calls for professional emergency assistance by contacting 911 or a local emergency number.
- Continues to provide care until more highly trained personnel arrive on the scene.

Although laws offer a degree of protection to a Good Samaritan, they are not necessarily a guarantee someone cannot or will not sue.

The Medical Reserve Corps website contains an overview of the Good Samaritan law, as well as a list of individual state statutes.[2] The National Conference of State Legislators website contains information regarding state laws related to AEDs.[3]

Q: What are our obligations to employees when there is a building emergency such as a water main break?

No federal or state laws specifically address this issue, but there are several factors to consider in the event of a water main break at an employer's location or building. Employee safety is the primary concern for an employer, followed by employee comfort.

In buildings with built-in sprinkler systems, city, municipality, or building codes may mandate a fully functioning sprinkler system in the buildings as long as there are human occupants. In the event of a water main break, there may not be enough water or pressure to deliver water when the sprinkler system is activated by smoke or fire. This can lead to a serious life-safety issue, and therefore, employees should be sent home immediately. Employers should work with their facilities personnel or building engineers to understand local laws and building codes.

Depending on the duration of the water main break outage, employers should also consider employees' access to toilet facilities. Occupational Safety and Health Administration (OSHA) standards require employers to make toilet facilities available so that employees can use them when they need to do so.[4] The employer may not impose unreasonable restrictions on employee use of the facilities.

The OSHA regulations define a toilet facility as "a fixed or portable facility designed for the purpose of adequate collection and containment of the products of both defecation and urination, which is [supplied] with toilet paper adequate to employee needs. Toilet facility includes biological, chemical, flush and combustion toilets and sanitary privies."[5]

Employers need to ensure that enough water pressure is available so that toilets can be cleanly and effectively flushed and that hand-washing facilities are functional. Without these facilities, the employer risks creating a health hazard.[6]

An option for employers with other buildings or office locations is to temporarily transfer employees to the other locations for the duration of the water main break rather than to send employees home. Employers should avoid sending employees to nonaffiliated neighborhood establishments or restaurants to "borrow" their toilet facilities, unless the neighborhood establishment agrees to it.

Employee safety is always the primary concern. If there is any doubt about the safety of employees as a result of the water main break, the best recourse is to send employees home.

Q: Should supervisors drive injured employees to the hospital, or should they simply call 911 and wait for first responders to arrive?

There is no clear answer to this question. It is up to the organization to make this determination, and there are pros and cons to both approaches.

A fairly common practice is for employers to refrain from allowing employees or supervisors to transport injured individuals to the hospital. There are several reasons an employer might prohibit doing so. For example, the employee's injury could be more serious than originally thought, or he or she could have an underlying medical condition that the supervisor is not aware of, leading to medical difficulties during the transport. The supervisor, who likely does not have medical training, would then be in the position of having to deal with a medical emergency while driving.

Some employers have a policy that advises supervisors to offer to contact 911 for emergency transportation or to get in touch with the injured individual's emergency contact to provide transportation to get medical attention. Obviously, the nature of the injury or illness should be taken into account when determining the best approach. Some employers automatically call for an ambulance for an injury in the workplace unless the employee signs a release declining such transportation.

Q: Is an employer liable when an employee on a company-sponsored sports team is injured during an event?

Sponsoring an employee sports team might seem like an innocuous way to boost employee morale and promote team building. But experts say it pays to assess and mitigate legal risks surrounding such events.

The first issue to consider is a possible workers' compensation claim if the employee is injured during an event. Workers' compensation laws vary from state to state, but in general, if an employee is injured playing on a company-sponsored team that is otherwise run by employees, the employee is not covered by workers' compensation because such benefits are typically paid for injuries suffered during the course of employment. There might be some exceptions, however, and employers can take certain steps to mitigate their risk.

It is possible for an employer to have liability as a property owner if it owns the facility where the activity takes place, or in some other nonemployer capacity, but such a scenario is unlikely.

The overriding question is whether an activity was conducted "in the course and scope of employment" or if the employer otherwise controlled the activity. If not, the employer is unlikely to be liable. However, if the employer is more closely involved in the activity, it could be liable for negligent supervision of its employees.

Companies can run into problems if they say that an event is voluntary but take actions that indicate the event is really not voluntary, such as noting in a performance evaluation that the employee did not participate. The employee's assumption then may be that participation is not voluntary but is required or beneficial to his or her future with the company.

In addition to any state workers' compensation-specific waiver form, organizations should work with legal counsel to design a general release stating that an activity is voluntary, that the company will exercise no supervision of the event, that the employee assumes the risk of any injury, and that the employee releases the company from any liability for injury sustained during the activity.

Below are some other guidelines for company-sponsored employee sports teams:

- Do not hold events on company property or during company time; do not allow employees to leave work early to attend games unless the employee chooses to do so under the usual time off policies.
- Make sure that the employee handbook is updated and details company policy about social events and athletic activities.
- Remind employees that normal work rules and standards apply to these types of activities.
- Remain aware of other nonemployer-sponsored recreational activities for employees such as a weekly pickup game of bas-

ketball among workers on your premises. Even if the company does not sponsor or pay for these activities, they could expose the employer to liability.

- Have zero tolerance for sexual harassment. Do not over-regulate sports teams, but if someone believes that they are being sexually harassed, take immediate action, as the risks for not doing so are high.

Chapter 6
General Safety and Security

Q: Must companies provide "sharps" containers for diabetic employees?

The Bloodborne Pathogens Standard of the Occupational Safety and Health Administration (OSHA) does not require an employer in a nonhealth care environment to provide a sharps container to an employee who uses needles and syringes for *personal therapeutic reasons.*[1]

Rather, the standard applies to all employees who have *occupational exposure* to blood or other potentially infectious materials. Therefore, employers should ensure the proper disposal of used needles and syringes. Discarded needles and syringes create a potential for exposure for other employees, in particular workers who empty the trash.

In addition, the Americans with Disabilities Act (ADA) does not require employers to provide a sharps container to employees. Reasonable accommodations are adjustments or modifications to the *workplace* or the *job* provided by an employer to enable people with disabilities to enjoy equal employment opportunities.

An employer has the responsibility for protecting all workers who may encounter discarded needles and syringes. This can be accomplished by requiring employees to discard their used needles and syringes in special containers. The employer may either provide the container or require the employee to bring in his or her own sharps container.

Q: Should a company provide over-the-counter medications to its employees?

Providing over-the-counter (OTC) medications to employees may expose an employer to liability or may even violate certain state laws, so caution is advised.

Though an aspirin, for example, may allow an employee with a headache to continue working and maintain productivity, even OTC medications have health risks and side effects that can be serious or possibly fatal. Also, some medications can cause drowsiness and result in a workplace accident.

Employers may suggest that employees take responsibility for their own OTC medications. This type of policy encourages employees to keep the one or two OTC medications they use at home in a locked desk or locker for times when they may need the medication. This option relieves the employer of any responsibility or liability for supplying medications, but it may not stop co-workers from sharing medications.

Another option (although many resources advise against this approach) is for employers to add one or two basic OTC medications to first-aid kits available to employees. If your company chooses to include OTC medications in a first-aid kit, provide only single-dose, tamper-evident packages that are properly labeled as regulated by the Food and Drug Administration. Do not purchase any product that contains ingredients known to cause drowsiness. With proper labeling, employees are then able to self-select if available OTC medications are right for them.

When making a decision to include OTC medications in first aid kits, your organization should proceed only after consultation with legal counsel and management. In addition, check any relevant state laws. For example, California's division of OSHA (CAL-OSHA) prohibits OTC medications from being included in first aid kits unless specifically approved by an employer-authorized, licensed physician.

Q: How can I ensure my company maintains the confidentiality of employees' personal data?

Companies must ensure that there are safeguards in place to protect personal employee information from theft. Identity theft has become a top consumer fraud issue, and the crime has been elevated to felony status. Every employer maintains records of great value to those who would engage in this illegal activity; therefore, employers should develop processes that protect the confidentiality of employee information. Employers should undertake periodic audits of their record-keeping processes to evaluate the safeguarding of employee records.

Employers can minimize identity theft by following some simple identification theft practices:

- Using a reliable shredder, shred all discarded employee information, including information on temporary workers, contract employees, and former employees.
- Keep personal employee and customer information locked up and secure at all times.
- Always be vigilant when employees have access to customer or employee information.
- Take the time to verify a new employee's Social Security number by contacting the Social Security Administration.
- Avoid using Social Security numbers as a form of identification for either employees or customers.
- Require health insurance carriers to use numbers other than Social Security numbers on health insurance cards.
- Build a firewall to keep employee and customer data from being e-mailed or faxed to other locations. Ask the information technology department if there is adequate protection from hackers.
- Designate someone to handle legitimate inquiries when necessary. Always ask the caller to provide a copy of a signed

release from the employee before verifying any information. Even then, confirm only the information that is needed.

- Ensure that the company collects only essential personal information from employees.
- Encourage employees to protect personal information at all times, even at home, and to keep only necessary personal information with them while at work.
- Have a plan ready and in position to act quickly should a theft or data breach occur.

Employers should remain abreast of state and federal employee record-keeping responsibilities. Some states have enacted laws related to the protection of Social Security numbers and personnel files. The Government Accountability Office provides a review of states with restrictions on private sector entities' use of Social Security numbers.[2] For international employers, the European Union has enacted new data standards that include the protection of employee records.

Q: We have had some vandalism in the employee bathrooms. What can we do to stop this?

Unfortunately, restrooms can be targets for employee vandalism. Employers can handle vandalism in various ways:

- Install surveillance equipment. Visible surveillance cameras outside the restrooms, especially cameras that record dates and times, can discourage vandals. The recordings provide evidence that may help identify the perpetrators. Seek legal counsel before installing such a system, and have employees sign forms acknowledging the existence of the cameras to help negate any reasonable expectation of privacy. Surveillance cameras should never be used inside a restroom.
- Add locks. Requiring a key to a locked facility can help

employers keep track of who used the restroom and when, and thereby determine who is most likely to have damaged the restroom. Another option is to use keycard access systems on the bathroom doors. As with surveillance, potential vandals would be less likely to engage in vandalism when they know the employer has a record of them using a restroom at a particular time.

- Improve maintenance. Frequent, immediate, and thorough attention to the cleanliness and repair of any damage to the restroom can reduce the likelihood of repeat behavior.

- Establish policies. Employers can create policies expressly prohibiting vandalism and requiring observed vandalism to be reported. Employees violating the policies can be disciplined in accordance with company disciplinary policies.

- Post etiquette rules. To ensure that everyone knows what behavior is expected, employers can post rules and recommendations for appropriate restroom etiquette inside the restrooms.

- Conduct surveys. Vandalism can be a symptom of larger problems, like diminished employee morale. Employers may want to conduct employee attitude surveys to get a sense of employees' thoughts and feelings regarding their work and workplace. Focus groups are another way to gather information from employees. Appropriate actions may then be taken to address any issues identified.

- Hire an attendant. Some employers may consider hiring temporary bathroom attendants to be stationed in or just outside the restrooms. Although the staffing costs could be hefty compared to the cost of cleaning up after vandalism, a live person can monitor restroom behavior much like a surveillance camera and can serve as a deterrent to vandalism.

Although there is no guarantee the vandalism will stop, these measures may help employers reduce the occurrence.

Q: What are some basic steps we can take to ensure our offices are safe for employees?

The first step a company should take in making this determination is to conduct a threat analysis of the worksite. This analysis involves a step-by-step, common-sense look at the workplace to find existing and potential threats to security. This process includes the following steps:

1. Review records to determine if there were any past incidents or security breaches.
2. Conduct an initial worksite inspection and analysis of the worksite.
3. Formulate a security plan.
4. Implement the plan.
5. Perform periodic audits to determine if gaps exist.

It is important to carefully select the person(s) who will perform the threat analysis, given that it is the foundation for a security program. Employers can delegate the responsibility to one person or to a team of employees. For large employers using a team approach, team members should be selected from different parts of the enterprise, such as senior management, operations, security, occupational safety and health, legal, human resources, and employees or union representatives. Smaller establishments might assign the responsibility to a single staff member or department, such as safety or human resources or to a consultant.

Some building security protocols to consider include the following:

- Install alarms, closed circuit television, or fencing.
- Hire security guards.

- Install building access control devices such as keycards.
- Control outside access to parking lots, or locate parking away from the building.
- Post security personnel in the parking garage, and issue vehicle identification decals.
- Ensure that vendors show proper company ID when accessing the building, and consider limiting access to approved vendors only.
- Provide an escort when contractors must access sensitive areas of the building.
- Determine the feasibility of sealing off entrances and exits when a threat situation occurs.
- Prevent public access to core building areas such as the mechanical room and roof.
- Pay particular attention to the security of lobbies, mailrooms, loading docks, and storage areas, as these can be particularly vulnerable.

Q: What are the essential elements of an effective safety and health program?

The elements of an effective safety and health program include the following:

- The active support of senior management, including the provision of required resources and access to qualified and competent professional personnel.
- Written safety responsibilities for line managers and supervisors, plus a commitment on their part to be accountable for workplace safety and health.
- The active involvement of employees in program design and operation.
- Written program goals, objectives, policies, procedures, implementation plans, and review processes that are com-

municated to employees. These written statements should be signed by the CEO or location manager to demonstrate management's commitment to the program. Employers should communicate this information to employees by bulletin board announcements, newsletters, meetings, e-mail, etc.

- A plan for dealing with hazards. The plan should be part of the program and should include hazard anticipation, recognition, evaluation, and abatement. To facilitate its use, the plan should provide for materials inventory, regular internal inspections, environmental monitoring, complaint investigations, and emergency procedures.

- Education and training focusing on the relevant and present hazards and on the responsibilities of management and employees in dealing with those hazards. Training in the use of relevant personal protective and response equipment should also be included.

- The review of OSHA's General Duty Clause[3] and specific standards to ensure the proper monitoring and assessment of hazards and of record maintenance.

- OSHA's requirements and state laws regarding the communication of hazards to employees and employee access to hazard data.

- The use of technologically feasible and cost-effective engineering controls, or the availability of personal protective equipment where such controls are not available.

Q: Can a company use video surveillance to monitor employees?

Video surveillance is one of many techniques employers can use to monitor employee activities in the workplace. Many employers use video surveillance to minimize theft, alcohol and drug use, and attendance problems and to identify unsafe working conditions.

Video monitoring can also provide evidence of a crime if one were to occur at the worksite. The legality of this type of surveillance depends on many factors. Employers must consider the laws for the state in which the surveillance occurs, whether the surveillance area is a public or private area, whether sound is provided in additional to the visual monitoring, and whether the camera is in open view or hidden.[4]

The Electronic Communications Privacy Act of 1986 is the primary federal law that addresses the issue of intercepting "electronic communication."[5] The law offers employers broad rights to monitor employees because silent video is exempted from the act. Employees seeking additional protection often seek help through applicable state privacy laws. Employers considering the use of video monitoring should contact legal counsel before establishing a surveillance policy and practice.

Q: May an employee record conversations with management and other employees without informing them?

The Omnibus Crime Control and Safe Streets Act of 1968,[6] amended by the Electronic Communications Privacy Act of 1986,[7] makes it unlawful to intentionally intercept wire, oral, or electronic communication. Often referred to as the Federal Wiretapping Act, the law allows an exception when one party to the conversation has consented to interception. Because the employee in question is a party to all conversations being recorded, federal law would not likely apply to this situation.

Some states require the consent of all parties to the communication to lawfully intercept communication.[8] Accordingly, secret recordings can be unlawful in those states, and violators can face fines and penalties if prosecuted.

Beyond complying with federal and state laws, employers may consider implementing a policy that prohibits employees from recording conversations.[9] Such a policy might include the following components:

- A statement regarding the purpose of the policy.
- Examples of the types of interception that are prohibited without authorization (such as tape recording, videotaping).
- A list of individuals in the organization who have the authority to allow any interception.
- Situations, if any, in which interception is permissible.
- Consequences of violating the policy.

Due to federal and state regulations involved, as well as existing and developing case law in this field, employers should consult with legal counsel in developing a policy regarding employee interception of communication in the workplace.

Chapter 7
Legal and Regulatory

Q: What are some effective practices for dealing with an OSHA inspection?

Employers should understand that an Occupational Safety and Health Administration (OSHA) inspector can visit an organization at any time, typically without advance notice. Most OSHA inspections happen for specific reasons; for example, an accident can trigger an OSHA inspection, as can an OSHA initiative targeted at a specific industry. Inspections can also occur because of an employee complaint regarding worker safety.

The types of violations an OSHA inspector might look for depend on the industry and the type of work being performed. Below is the list of the most frequently cited OSHA violations in fiscal year 2013.[1]

- Construction
  - » Scaffolding, general requirements.
  - » Fall protection.
  - » Ladders.
- General industry:
  - » Hazard communication standard.
  - » Respiratory protection.
  - » Control of hazardous energy (lockout/tagout).
  - » Electrical, wiring methods, components, and equipment.
  - » Powered industrial trucks.
  - » Electrical systems design, general requirements.
  - » Machines, general requirements.

Given that OSHA does not issue a warning before an inspection takes place, it is critical for a company to ensure its compliance with OSHA regulations. Periodic self-audits and OSHA audit checklists are extremely helpful in making certain a company is following OSHA regulations.

At the time of the inspection, an effective practice is to designate a member of management as the key contact for monitoring the inspection and dealing with the inspector. Responsibilities include the following:

- Designating the area for opening and closing conferences.
- Attending the opening and closing conferences.
- Accompanying the OSHA inspector during the inspection.
- Being prepared to respond to OSHA's document requests by providing OSHA 300 logs, 300A forms, and other safety-related documents.
- Ensuring that employees are aware of their rights during an OSHA interview.
- Ensuring that a partial inspection does not suddenly develop into a "wall-to-wall" inspection and that the inspection does not interfere with the company's production.
- Promptly correcting violations once the inspection is completed.
- Communicating with legal counsel about legal issues that may arise, such as search warrants or subpoenas.
- Along with company legal counsel, firmly exercising the company's legal rights.
- At the closing conference, taking notes and asking how long the company has to address any violations.

Q: Are all companies required to post OSHA Form 300A, the Summary of Work-Related Injuries and Illnesses?

No. Certain industries are exempt from OSHA's record-keeping requirements. Employers with 10 or fewer employees during all of the calendar year are not required to post OSHA Form 300A. In addition, businesses classified in specific low-hazard retail, service, finance, insurance, or real estate industries are not required to keep injury and illness records unless the Bureau of Labor Statistics or OSHA informs them in writing that they must do so.

Establishments classified in the following Standard Industrial Codes (SIC) are exempt from most of the OSHA record-keeping requirements, regardless of size:

- 525 Hardware Stores
- 542 Meat and Fish Markets
- 544 Candy, Nut, and Confectionary Stores
- 545 Dairy Products Stores
- 546 Retail Bakeries
- 549 Miscellaneous Food Stores
- 551 New and Used Car Dealers
- 552 Used Car Dealers
- 554 Gasoline Service Stations
- 557 Motorcycle Dealers
- 56 Apparel and Accessory Stores
- 573 Radio, Television, and Computer Stores
- 58 Eating and Drinking Places
- 591 Drug Stores and Proprietary Stores
- 592 Liquor Stores
- 594 Miscellaneous Shopping Goods Stores
- 599 Retail Stores, Not Elsewhere Classified
- 60 Depository Institutions (Banks and Savings Institutions)
- 61 Nondepository Institutions (Credit Institutions)
- 62 Security and Commodity Brokers
- 63 Insurance Carriers
- 64 Insurance Agents, Brokers and Services
- 653 Real Estate Agents and Managers
- 654 Title Abstract Offices

- 67 Holding and Other Investment Offices
- 722 Photographic Studios, Portrait
- 723 Beauty Shops
- 724 Barber Shops
- 725 Shoe Repair and Shoeshine Parlors
- 726 Funeral Service and Crematories
- 729 Miscellaneous Personal Services
- 731 Advertising Services
- 732 Credit Reporting and Collection Services
- 733 Mailing, Reproduction, and Stenographic Services
- 737 Computer and Data Processing Services
- 738 Miscellaneous Business Services
- 764 Reupholstery and Furniture Repair
- 78 Motion Picture
- 791 Dance Studios, Schools, and Halls
- 792 Producers, Orchestras, Entertainers
- 793 Bowling Centers
- 801 Offices and Clinics of Medical Doctors
- 802 Offices and Clinics of Dentists
- 803 Offices of Osteopathic Physicians
- 804 Offices of Other Health Practitioners
- 807 Medical and Dental Laboratories
- 809 Health and Allied Services, Not Elsewhere Classified
- 81 Legal Services
- 82 Educational Services (Schools, Colleges, Universities, and Libraries)
- 832 Individual and Family Services
- 835 Child Day Care Centers
- 839 Social Services, Not Elsewhere Classified
- 841 Museums and Art Galleries
- 86 Membership Organizations
- 87 Engineering, Accounting, Research, Management, and Related Services
- 899 Services, Not Elsewhere Classified.

Each employer covered by the Occupational Safety and Health (OSH) Act *must* report to OSHA any workplace incident resulting in a fatality or the in-patient hospitalization of three or more employees within eight hours. This is a separate requirement than the OSHA 300 reporting requirement.

Q: Does OSHA require companies to keep their workplaces at a certain temperature?

Not necessarily. There is no requirement for employers to maintain a certain workplace temperature under federal OSHA regulations; however, OSHA does recommend employers maintain workplace temperatures in the range of 68 to 76 degrees Fahrenheit and humidity control in the range of 20 to 60 percent. According to a 2003 OSHA interpretation letter, "Office temperature and humidity conditions are generally a matter of human comfort rather than hazards that could cause death or serious physical harm. OSHA cannot cite the General Duty Clause for personal discomfort."[2]

Indoor air temperature preferences vary by individual. Though one worker may shiver and reach for a sweater during the summer with the thermostat set on 70 degrees, another worker may break a sweat. Finding a happy medium can often be difficult, but consider the bottom line: a 2004 study by Cornell University found that 77 degrees is the optimum temperature for office employee productivity.[3] "At 77 degrees Fahrenheit, the workers were keyboarding 100 percent of the time with a 10 percent error rate, but at 68 degrees, their keying rate went down to 54 percent of the time with a 25 percent error rate," the study reports. "Temperature is certainly a key variable that can impact performance," the study concludes.

Aside from productivity, office temperature can also have a negative effect on morale, and allowing employees some flexibility in regulating indoor temperature can increase job satisfaction.

Q: Does the Occupational Safety & Health Act cover all employers?

The OSH Act of 1970 is administered by OSHA. In general, the act covers all employers and their employees in the 50 states, the District of Columbia, Puerto Rico, and other U.S. territories. Coverage is provided either directly by the federal OSHA or by an OSHA-approved state job safety and health plan. Employees of the U.S. Postal Service are also covered.

The act defines an employer as any "person engaged in a business affecting commerce who has employees, but does not include the United States or any state or political subdivision of a State." Therefore, the act applies to employers and employees in such varied fields as manufacturing, construction, longshoring, agriculture, law and medicine, charity and disaster relief, organized labor, and private education. The act establishes a separate program for federal government employees and extends coverage to state and local government employees only through the states with OSHA-approved plans.[4] The act does not cover:

- Self-employed persons.
- Farms that employ only immediate members of the farmer's family.
- Working conditions for which other federal agencies, operating under the authority of other federal laws, regulate worker safety. This category includes most working conditions in mining, nuclear energy, and nuclear weapons manufacture, and many aspects of the transportation industries.
- Employees of state and local governments, unless they are in one of the states operating an OSHA-approved state plan.

Q: What are OSHA standards?

OSHA standards are rules that describe the methods that employers must use to protect their employees from hazards. There are OSHA standards for construction work,[5] maritime operations,[6] and general industry,[7] which is the set that applies to most worksites. These standards limit the amount of hazardous chemicals workers can be exposed to, require the use of certain safe practices and equipment, and require employers to monitor hazards and keep records of workplace injuries and illnesses. Examples of OSHA standards include requirements to provide fall protection, prevent trenching cave-ins, prevent infectious diseases, ensure that workers safely enter confined spaces, prevent exposure to harmful substances like asbestos, put guards on machines, provide respirators or other safety equipment, and provide training for certain dangerous jobs.

Employers must also comply with the General Duty Clause[8] of the OSH Act, which requires employers to keep their workplace free of serious recognized hazards. This clause is generally cited when no OSHA standard applies to the hazard.

Q: What are OSHA's reporting requirements for fatalities or multiple hospitalizations?

The U.S. Department of Labor (DOL) requires employers to notify OSHA within eight hours of an incident that involves a fatality or the hospitalization of three or more employees.[9] Employers should note that state laws may require notification to a state agency within a shorter period of time.[10] Although a fatality or the hospitalization of three or more employees does not necessarily mean a violation has occurred, OSHA is required to inspect for hazardous work conditions. All employers are subject to the eight-hour notification rule.

For an employer to provide an oral report to OSHA on a fatality or multiple hospitalizations, a company representative must take one of the following actions:

- Call the OSHA area office nearest to the accident site.
- Notify, in person, the OSHA area office nearest to the accident site.

- Call the OSHA central phone number, (800) 321-OSHA (6742).

Because OSHA requires prompt notification, these three methods are the only acceptable ones that comply with the regulations. In addition to an employer providing an oral notification, the company can fax, mail, or hand deliver the required information as a backup measure.

When an employer makes a report of a fatality or multiple hospitalizations, the following information must be included:

- Name of the establishment
- Location of the incident
- Time of the incident
- Number of fatalities or hospitalized employees
- Contact person
- Telephone number
- Brief description of the incident

If an incident is followed by a fatality or the hospitalization of three or more employees within 30 days of the incident, the employer is required to provide the same notification within eight hours of learning of the fatality or hospitalization.

Q: What are OSHA's requirements under the bloodborne pathogens standard?

OSHA implemented the Bloodborne Pathogens Standard (BPS) in 1992. The standard protects all employees in positions where it is "reasonably anticipated" that the employee will be exposed to blood or other potentially infected bodily fluids. Though the vast majority of protected workers are in the health care industry, the standard also covers employees in linen services, medical equipment repair, emergency technicians, funeral services, and other industries.

The BPS can be divided into two categories: risk management and record-keeping. Under the risk management requirements, an employer must:

- Implement universal precautions.
- Have a written exposure control plan.
- Have exposure control procedures.
- Provide personal protective equipment.
- Provide training and hazard communication.
- Provide free hepatitis B vaccinations.
- Provide free post-exposure incident medical evaluations, lab tests, treatment, and counseling.
- Employee participation (health care): Relative to employee participation, it is important for employers to solicit input from nonmanagerial employees responsible for direct patient care who are potentially exposed from contaminated sharps in identification, evaluation, and selection of effective engineering and work practice controls.

Under the record-keeping requirements, an employer must:

- Maintain exposure records for the duration of the exposed employee's employment, plus 30 years.
- Record needle sticks (if medical treatment is necessary) on Form OSHA 200.
- Maintain training records for three years.
- Maintain sharps injury log.

OSHA has developed a fact sheet on the BPS.[11]

Q: Does OSHA require companies to provide toilet facilities for employees?

OSHA's sanitation standard for general industry requires employers to provide their employees with toilet facilities.[12]

The regulations state that "toilet facilities, in toilet rooms separate for each sex, shall be provided in all places of employment in accordance with [Table 6.1] of this section. The number of facilities to be provided for each sex shall be based on the number of employees of that sex for whom the facilities are furnished. Where toilet rooms will be occupied by no more than one person at a time, can be locked from the inside, and contain at least one water closet, separate toilet rooms for each sex need not be provided. Where such single-occupancy rooms have more than one toilet facility, only one such facility in each toilet room shall be counted for the purpose of [Table 6.1]."

Table 6.1 I Number of Toilet Facilities Per Employee	
Number of employees	Minimum number of water closets[a]
1 to 15	1
16 to 35	2
36 to 55	3
56 to 80	4
81 to 110	5
111 to 150	6
Over 150	b
Notes:	
[a]Where toilet facilities will not be used by women, urinals may be provided instead of water closets, except that the number of water closets in such cases shall not be reduced to less than 2/3 of the minimum specified.	
[b]One additional fixture for each additional 40 employees.	

For farm workers and other agriculture employees, the field sanitation standard for agriculture mandates that toilets be located no more than a quarter mile walk from the location where employees are working.[13] Toilet facility means "a fixed or portable facility designed for the purpose of adequate collection and containment of the products of both defecation and urination which is [supplied] with toilet paper adequate to employee needs. Toilet facility includes biological, chemical, flush and combustion toilets and sanitary privies." There must be at least one toilet facility and one hand-washing facility for each 20 employees or fraction thereof, unless the field-work employees work for a period of three hours or less (including transportation time to and from the field) during the day.

Furthermore, each facility needs to occupy a separate compartment with a door and walls or partitions between fixtures that are high enough to assure privacy. Facilities must have hot and cold or tepid running water. Hand soap or similar cleansing agents need to be provided. Individual hand towels or sections of cloth or paper, warm air blowers, or clean individual sections of continuous cloth toweling that are convenient to the lavatories must also be provided.

Employers should also have a back-up plan in the event a company location loses access to water (that is, a broken water line). In that event, the employer should notify employees of the temporary interruption in service and should bring in portable restrooms or allow employees who may need to use the facilities to go to a nearby establishment for this purpose. When doing so, employees should be instructed to notify their supervisors before leaving the premises.

Q: What is a recordable injury for purposes of OSHA reporting?

For an injury or illness to be recordable, it must be work-related. An injury is considered work-related if an event or exposure in the workplace caused or contributed to the condition or significantly aggravated a preexisting condition.

Injuries not work-related include those sustained by the general public, certain parking lot accidents, nonwork-induced mental illnesses, colds or flu, injuries that arise from personal meals or grooming, injuries that are self-inflicted or from self-medication, and those occurring on the premises due to outside factors (such as a natural disaster).

Generally, a recordable injury or illness under OSHA is one that requires medical treatment beyond first aid, as well as one that causes death, days away from work, restricted work, transfer to another job, or loss of consciousness. Time spent at the initial doctor visit for observation or diagnostics to determine if an injury or illness is present is not considered medical treatment beyond first aid. According to OSHA, "A significant injury or illness diagnosed by a physician or other licensed health care professional, even if it does not result in death, days away from work, restricted work or job transfer, medical treatment beyond first-aid, or loss of consciousness," must also be recorded.[14]

First aid treatments include the following:

- Using a nonprescription medication at nonprescription strength. (For medications available in both prescription and nonprescription form, a recommendation by a physician or other licensed health care professional to use a nonprescription medication at prescription strength is considered medical treatment for record-keeping purposes.)
- Administering tetanus immunizations. (Other immunizations, such as hepatitis B vaccine or rabies vaccine, are considered medical treatment.)
- Cleaning, flushing, or soaking wounds on the surface of the skin.
- Using wound coverings such as bandages, Band-Aids™, gauze pads, butterfly bandages or Steri-Strips™. (Other wound closing devices such as sutures and staples are considered medical treatment.)
- Using hot or cold therapy.
- Using any nonrigid means of support, such as elastic bandages, wraps, or nonrigid back belts. (Devices with rigid stays

or other systems designed to immobilize parts of the body are considered medical treatment for record-keeping purposes.)

- Using temporary immobilization devices while transporting an accident victim (for example, splints, slings, neck collars, back boards).
- Drilling of a fingernail or toenail to relieve pressure, or draining fluid from a blister.
- Using eye patches.
- Removing foreign bodies from the eye using only irrigation or a cotton swab.
- Removing splinters or foreign material from areas other than the eye by irrigation, tweezers, cotton swabs, or other simple means.
- Using finger guards.
- Using massages. (Physical therapy or chiropractic treatment is considered medical treatment for record-keeping purposes.)
- Drinking fluids for relief of heat stress.

The OSHA regulations on recordable injuries and illnesses are listed in 29 C.F.R. Sections 1904.8 through 1904.12.[15]

Q: What is the process for OSHA inspections?

Every establishment covered by the OSH Act of 1970 is subject to inspection by OSHA compliance safety and health officers (CSHOs).[16] These occupational safety and health professionals possess the knowledge and experience required to conduct workplace inspections. They have been thoroughly trained in recognizing safety and health hazards and in enforcing OSHA's standards. In states with their own OSHA-approved state plan, pursuant to state law, state officials conduct inspections, issue citations for violations, and propose penalties in a manner that is at least as effective as the federal program.

OSHA conducts two general types of inspections: programmed and unprogrammed. Establishments with high injury rates receive programmed inspections, whereas unprogrammed inspections are used in response to fatalities, catastrophes, and complaints, which are further addressed by OSHA's complaint policies and procedures. Various OSHA publications and documents detail OSHA's policies and procedures for inspections, including OSHA's Field Operations Manual.[17]

Q: What types of violations does OSHA treat, and what are their associated penalties?

The OSH Act of 1970 authorizes OSHA to treat certain violations, which have no direct or immediate relationship to safety and health, as *de minimus*, requiring no penalty or abatement. OSHA does not issue citations for *de minimus* violations. OSHA does, however levy fines for the following types of violations.

- Other than serious violation: A violation that has a direct relationship to job safety and health, but probably would not cause death or serious physical harm. A proposed penalty of up to $7,000 for each violation is discretionary.
- Serious violation: A violation where a substantial probability that death or serious physical harm could result and where the employer knew, or should have known, of the hazard. A penalty of up to $7,000 for each violation must be proposed.
- Willful violation: A violation that the employer intentionally and knowingly commits. The employer either knows that what it is doing constitutes a violation, or is aware that a condition creates a hazard and has made no reasonable effort to eliminate it. The Act provides that an employer who willfully violates the Act may be assessed a civil penalty of not more than $70,000 but not less than $5,000 for each violation. Proposed penalties for other-than-serious and seri-

ous violations may be adjusted downward depending on the employer's good faith (demonstrated efforts to comply with the Act through the implementation of an effective health and safety program), history of violations, and size of business. Proposed penalties for willful violations may be adjusted downward depending on the size of the business. Usually no credit is given for good faith. If an employer is convicted of a willful violation of a standard that has resulted in the death of an employee, the offense is punishable by a court-imposed fine or by imprisonment for up to six months, or both. A fine of up to $250,000 for an individual, or $500,000 for an organization authorized under the Omnibus Crime Control Act of 1984, not the OSH Act may be imposed for a criminal conviction.

- Repeat violation. A violation of any standard, regulation, rule, or order where, upon re-inspection, a substantially similar violation is found. Repeat violations can bring fines of up to $70,000 for each such violation. To serve as the basis for a repeat citation, the original citation must be final; a citation under contest may not serve as the basis for a subsequent repeat citation.
- Failure to abate violation. Failure to correct a prior violation may bring a civil penalty of up to $7,000 for each day the violation continues beyond the prescribed abatement date.

Citation and penalty procedures may differ somewhat in states with their own OSH programs.

Q: What is the purpose of the OSHA 300 log?

The OSHA Log (otherwise known as the Form 300) is used to classify work-related injuries and illnesses and to note the extent and severity of each case.[18] When an incident occurs, the form is used to record specific details about what happened and how it happened. The Summary—a separate form (otherwise known as the Form 300A)—shows the totals for the year in each category.[19] At the end of the year, covered employers must post the Summary in a visible location so that employees are aware of the injuries and illnesses occurring in their workplace. Employers must keep an OSHA Log for each establishment or site. Companies with multiple locations must keep a separate Log and Summary for each physical location that is expected to be in operation for one year or longer.

Q: What training does OSHA require?

The OSH Act of 1970 does not specifically address the responsibility of employers to provide health and safety information and instruction to employees. However, more than 100 of the act's current standards do contain training requirements.

OSHA has developed voluntary training guidelines to assist employers in providing the safety and health information and instruction needed for their employees to work at minimal risk to themselves, to fellow employees, and to the public. These guidelines, as well as guidelines on general industry training requirements, can be found on the OSHA website.[20]

Q: Are companies required to comply with FBI or local police requests for information?

In general, law enforcement officials are allowed to request certain types of information from employers without a court order. However, there may be legal implications for a company that provides employee information without first checking state laws, as some state laws include provisions on the disclosure of employment-related information to third parties.

In most cases, these laws require employees' written consent for disclosure of information, but not if the information is limited to verification of employment dates, title or position, and salary, or if disclosure is required by court order.

When law enforcement officials request employee information, it is crucial to involve the point person designated by the company to receive and evaluate such requests. This point of contact is usually the company's legal counsel.

If there is no subpoena, but the request is for limited information such as employment dates, title or position, or salary, employers should first check company policy, then make the determination to provide the information.

When law enforcement officials have a subpoena, the company can either comply with the subpoena or have legal counsel apply to the court to vacate or modify the subpoena.

Employers may wish to add a disclaimer to their current policies alerting employees to the possible need to disclose confidential information if requested by the federal government.

Q: What are the liabilities of serving alcohol at a holiday party? How can companies minimize liability?

One of the most common concerns during an organization's holiday party or other seasonal celebration is serving alcohol. The legal issue is whether an employer is liable if an employee subsequently drives under the influence and causes an accident that injures the employee or others.

The law on this issue varies from state to state. However, some general guidelines can be gleaned from court cases.

The greatest exposure to employers is if they serve alcohol to minors. If a minor is involved in an accident while driving under the influence of alcohol served to him or her by the employer, it is likely that the employer will be held liable as a "social host."

The result is less clear when the employee is an adult. In some states, "social host" liability is restricted to the service of alcohol to minors. However, even in such states, the case law often leaves open the possibility that employers may potentially be held liable.

Moreover, even where there is no potential for legal liability, there are moral considerations. It would be hard to sleep at night if you knew that a serious or fatal accident involving one of your employees might have been avoided had reasonable steps been taken to limit the consumption of alcohol.

Obviously, the safest approach, from a legal perspective, is to supply no alcohol. However, this may not be practical or desirable.

Where alcohol is provided, the following guidelines should help minimize the employer's risk:

- Make clear in pre-party communications that minors cannot drink and that if they do, they may be terminated. Ask those who dispense the alcohol to keep an eye out for those who look too young to drink and to card individuals if they have any doubt.
- Make clear in pre-party communications that employees must limit their consumption to avoid being under the influence.
- Have someone serve alcohol rather than permit employees to serve themselves. Doing so not only gives the servers (the number of which should be limited) the opportunity to flag employees who drink too much, but it may also deter employees from pouring too many drinks in the first place.
- Consider establishing a maximum number of drinks that individuals can have. Tickets do not work because individuals can give away their tickets. Consider a fluorescent stamp on an employee's hand in exchange for a drink, limiting the number of stamps an employee can receive.
- Make cab vouchers available to employees, and ensure they can obtain vouchers without going to a manager.

- Provide a variety of entertainment (for example, dancing, games) so that drinking is not the focus of the party.
- Hold the party at a location that is easily accessible by public transportation.
- Ask certain managers to keep their eyes and ears open for individuals who are visibly intoxicated.
- Serve plenty of nonalcoholic beverages and lots of food.
- Consider using sober/safe ride programs.[21]
- If the party is held at a hotel, arrange for a block of rooms that employees can reserve at a discount.

Q: What is a NAICS code used for?

The North American Industry Classification System (NAICS) was developed as the standard for use by federal statistical agencies in classifying business establishments for the collection, analysis, and publication of statistical data related to the business economy of the United States.[22] NAICS was developed under the auspices of the Office of Management and Budget (OMB) and adopted in 1997 to replace the old SIC system. It was also developed in cooperation with the statistical agencies of Canada and Mexico to establish a three-country standard that allows for a high level of comparability in business statistics among the three countries. Certain government departments and agencies, such as the U.S. Securities and Exchange Commission (SEC), still use the SIC codes.

Labor force trends can be tracked using data collected by NAICS code. Data organized under NAICS are also used to assess equal employment opportunity (EEO) in various industries and to help employers around the country prepare affirmative action plans. Data collected under NAICS is helpful in many kinds of research, such as the identification of industries that may expose people to harmful chemicals or other health and safety hazards.

Q: Can an employer ask employees what type of medication they are taking and why?

The Americans with Disabilities Act (ADA) does not protect just disabled individuals; it also protects the privacy of medical information of applicants and employees, disabled or not.

Questions regarding prescription drug use may be considered a medical-related inquiry under the ADA. Therefore, employer inquiries regarding the use of prescription medications may be prohibited under the ADA in all but a few circumstances.

The U.S. Equal Employment Opportunity Commission (EEOC) has issued guidance explaining the exceptions to the medical inquiries limitations.[23] The guidance states that in general, employers may not ask all employees about the prescription drugs they take. Asking all employees about their use of prescription drugs is rarely job-related and consistent with business necessity. Therefore, only a handful of occupations will be able to demonstrate that prescription-related inquiries would be job-related and consistent with business necessity. The example the EEOC provides is police officers. In occupations of this type, because of the significant safety risk involved with the use of certain prescription medications, employers may be able to demonstrate that asking employees about their prescription drug use is job-related and consistent with business necessity. Conversely, administrative positions such as accountants, information technology professionals, administrative assistants, HR professionals, and most management positions would not face significant job-related safety risks associated with side effects caused by prescription medications.

Unfortunately, the EEOC does not provide a list of additional occupations that would meet the medical inquiries limitation exceptions. As a result, it is not clear whether this type of exception would similarly apply to hazardous occupations such as operators of heavy machinery. Employers therefore need to consult with legal counsel about whether other occupations meet this exception to the law.

There are also exceptions pertaining to medical inquiries for occupations regulated by federal law. For example, a provision of the Federal Motor Carrier Safety Act indicates that drivers in safety-sensitive positions may be required to disclose the use of controlled substances, though there are some exceptions to this rule.[24] Similarly, the Federal Aviation Administration has issued guidance requiring pilots and other aircraft-related, safety-sensitive positions to disclose prescribed medications.[25]

For the vast majority of positions, employers may not ask job applicants about prescription drug use, regardless of the job, prior to making an offer of employment. Pending further direction from the EEOC on this topic, employers that feel it is necessary to have policies regarding employee prescription drug use should have them reviewed by legal counsel.

Q: What resources are available that provide ergonomic advice or recommendations for workplace modifications and design?

OSHA provides information on ergonomics issues and workplace measures to reduce the possibility of repetitive stress injuries.[26] The National Institute for Occupational Safety and Health (NIOSH) also maintains a website with information and scientific research on ergonomics.[27]

In addition, the website of the International Ergonomics Association (IEA) provides information and opportunities to interact on international issues relating to the science of ergonomics.[28]

The Human Factors and Ergonomics Society provides free resources, tips, and links to aid members and nonmembers in educating and training themselves and others about the human factors/ergonomics (HF/E) field.[29]

Information to facilitate the design, modification, or management of work processes is part of an ergonomics guideline developed by the American Society for Testing and Materials.[30]

Chapter 8
Technology

Q: What are some best-practice approaches to safeguard employee data?

The HR department has long been the protector of sensitive employee information, keeping it under literal lock and key with restricted access given on a need-to-know basis. Increasingly, this type of information is being stored in web-based formats, accessible to those with the correct credentials from any device with Internet connectivity. Listed below are some best-practice approaches to help ensure the security of confidential employee information.

- Tighten password use. In addition to securing information online, require employees to put passwords on all devices they use to access sensitive company information.[1] This includes laptops, smartphones, and iPads. Passwords help protect information that is left open by locking out the device after a certain period of time. Employers may take this a step further and require regular rotation of passwords and specify a level of complexity for the password (for example, a combination of symbols, letters, and numbers).

- Educate employees on policy. Create a policy that discusses the use of mobile devices, both corporately owned and personal.[2] Educate new employees on this policy early in employment, and communicate it to all employees regularly. The policy should address employee responsibility regarding sensitive information accessed on mobile devices and protocols the company will follow if sensitive information is breached.[3] This policy may also require employees to disclose personal devices they use to access confidential corporate information.

- Engage IT staff to enforce and monitor. Although employees should take personal responsibility for accessing sensitive information, employers should also equip IT with the tools necessary to monitor employee access. When an employer suspects that information is being used or accessed inappropriately, have protocols in place to give certain IT staff the authority to restrict access until the matter is investigated thoroughly.

- Use technology solutions. Technology exists to help employers guard sensitive data, regardless of the device used to access it. This includes systems that prohibit employees from copying and pasting material from a secure web browser into a document on a personal laptop. Other technology can remotely delete data from a device should it be lost or stolen, or if an invalid password is entered a certain number of times. Employers should also consider investing in IT development, so that the company is aware of new cyber threats and employees are trained to handle them.

- Understand relevant laws. A number of states have enacted laws that require notification to individuals whose sensitive personal information has been breached. Additionally, many foreign countries have stringent rules regarding employers monitoring employees' personal devices. HR professionals should understand all relevant laws and bring their organization's policies into compliance.

Q: Can an employer remotely wipe/brick an employee's personal cellphone?

As more and more companies are implementing "bring your own

device" (BYOD) policies, there is increased concern over lost personal cellphones or unhappy former employees with sensitive and confidential company data. As a result, employers are taking what may appear to be an extreme measure to protect this data. One such measure is implementing a "remote wipe" of company and employee personal cellphones. Certainly, the ability to wipe a company-issued cellphone would be permissible. Questions arise when the discussion turns to employees' personal cellphones and wiping both personal and company data from a device. Currently, this practice is not prohibited under state and federal regulations. However, employers should implement such policies cautiously.

The more employees use smartphones and other personal electronic devices to access company information, data, and documents, the more important it is for a company to have policies and processes in place to ensure the security of its data. For example, an employer can require that all personal devices and smartphones have password access protections or firewalls in place. However, these protections are, at times, insufficient. Therefore, employers are beginning to include a remote wipe provision within their policies.

Cellphone wiping provisions are typically included within a company cellphone policy or within a company property acknowledgement form. There is also a growing trend to include a remote wipe provision as part of a well-crafted BYOD policy. Typically, such a policy would require employees to download mobile device management software. This software is available for a variety of platforms, including iPhone, Android, and Windows, to name a few. Typically, all that is required is a connection to the company's e-mail system. A message is then sent to a lost or stolen cellphone from the company e-mail system, and all data is wiped from the device, including company and personal data maintained on the device.

A well-crafted policy should clearly address how IT and the company will manage employees' personal devices, including what steps will be taken when a device is lost or stolen and what will happen at the time of termination. Employers should also have employees sign an authorization to wipe data from the phone prior to allowing them to access company data under a BYOD policy.

As state and federal regulations struggle to keep up with new technology, an employer's ability to wipe employee personal cellphones and devices will likely be tested through the courts in the future. Employers must stay up to date on rulings and proposed legislation.[4] In addition, international companies should review the applicable laws in each country prior to implementing a remote wipe policy or practice.

Chapter 9
Violence

Q: What should an employer do when domestic violence spills over into the workplace?

Domestic violence affects the workplace in numerous ways. Domestic violence, when it spills over into the workplace, can lead to increased absenteeism, turnover, higher health care costs, and sharply decreased productivity. The U.S. Centers for Disease Control and Prevention found that the cost of domestic violence is $5.8 billion annually.[1]

Often, victims do not tell HR or managers that they are being abused. But if an employer suspects that an employee might be the victim of domestic abuse and that the abuser might attempt to harm the employee or others at the workplace, the employer must take steps to protect the workforce. Under the General Duty Clause[2] of the Occupational Safety and Health (OSH) Act, employers are required to take "feasible steps to minimize risks" in workplaces where "the risk of violence and significant personal injury are significant enough to be 'recognized hazards,'" according to an Occupational Safety and Health Administration (OSHA) letter of interpretation.[3]

ASIS International and the Society for Human Resource Management have collaborated to develop a *Workplace Violence Prevention and Intervention Standard*.[4] The standard provides an overview of policies, processes, and protocols organizations can adopt to identify and prevent threatening behavior and violence affecting the workplace, and to better address and resolve threats and violence that have occurred. The standard contains a section with guidance on dealing with domestic violence in the workplace.

Managers and supervisors who suspect an employee might be the victim of domestic abuse should look for a pattern of the following behaviors:

- Absenteeism or lateness, poor concentration, and work-related errors or inconsistent work product that is not characteristic of the employee.
- Injuries, especially repeated injuries, such as bruises, black eyes, and broken bones, especially if the employee attempts to conceal the injuries or offers unconvincing explanation for how they occurred.
- Requests for time off to attend court appearances.
- Signs of emotional distress, such as unusual quietness and increased isolation from co-workers and unusual or repeated emotional upset during or following contact with the employee's partner.
- Suggestions or statements by the employee that a former or current partner is engaging in unwanted contact.
- An unusual number of e-mails, texts or phone calls from a current or former partner and reluctance by the employee to converse with the partner or respond to messages.
- Abrupt change of address by the employee or a reluctance to divulge where the employee resides.
- Unwelcome visits by the employee's partner to the workplace, particularly if the visits elicit a strong negative reaction by the employee.

Employers can help victims of domestic violence by taking the following steps:

- Encourage the use of the company employee assistance program or community resources focused on domestic violence. HR professionals should avoid trying to counsel the person.
- In states that permit employers to obtain restraining orders covering the workplace, evaluate the feasibility of obtaining such an order when threats from an employee's abusive partner affect the workplace.
- Limit or bar the abuser's access to the workplace, such as distributing the abuser's photograph to security personnel, members of management, or the employee's workgroup.
- Take additional security steps such as providing an escort to the parking lot, providing a parking space close to the building, offering flexible or varied work hours, removing the employee's name from the office directory, screening calls, and changing the employee's work e-mail address.

If the employee refuses help or denies that any abuse is going on, but the employer still suspects that the employee is being abused and that the abuser might come to the workplace, then the employer still has a responsibility to protect the employee and co-workers on the premises.

Employers should be aware that several states have passed laws protecting the workplace rights of victims of domestic or sexual violence.[5] Before taking any type of action against an employee suspected of being the victim of domestic violence, employers should carefully check the laws in the states where they do business. Even in states that have not passed such laws, employers should establish written policies on leave requests and related issues.

Q: How does an employer handle a situation when a married couple work together, have filed for divorce, and

one spouse has an order of protection against the other spouse?

Employers should keep in mind that the OSH Act's General Duty Clause[6] has a requirement to provide a safe environment for all employees. If an employer is put on notice that domestic violence exists and the threats are affecting employees at the workplace, the employer must act on that knowledge. If an employer mishandles this situation, it can result in enormous liability.

A *SHRM Legal Report* article provides comprehensive guidelines for managers to follow to have the most successful outcome in this situation.[7] The article outlines the steps to follow after learning of a protection order and discusses recommended actions, including alternate work arrangements.

In addition, ASIS International and SHRM collaborated to develop a *Workplace Violence Prevention and Intervention Standard*.[8] The standard provides an overview of policies, processes, and protocols organizations can adopt to identify and prevent threatening behavior and violence affecting the workplace, and to better address and resolve threats and violence that have occurred.

Q: How can an employer help an employee whom the employer suspects is the victim of domestic violence?

Victims of domestic violence often do not tell their supervisors or HR professionals that they are being abused out of fear or shame. If abuse is suspected, watch for these warning signs:

- Wears long sleeves or sunglasses at inappropriate times to conceal injuries
- Startles easily
- Arrives early or late to work
- Appears fatigued
- Exhibits fear, anxiety, or depression
- Has unexplained injuries

- Shows a decrease in productivity
- Takes more unplanned time off

Employers can help abuse victims by directing them to experts in the company's employee assistance program or local shelters. Avoid trying to counsel the person directly.

Other ways in which an employer can help include the following:

- Ask the employee what changes in the work environment would make her or him feel safer, such as providing priority parking and escorts from the parking area.
- Change the employee's office phone number, and remove the employee's name from automated contact lists. Install panic buttons for the employee and receptionist.
- Place plants or partitions around the employee's work area to serve as barricades to prevent the abuser from walking directly up to the employee. Notify the police.
- Save any threatening messages received at the workplace for future legal action. Provide time off or flexible work hours for counseling and court appearances.
- Ask the employee to obtain a restraining order that includes the workplace, and keep a copy on hand.

If the employee refuses to contact police or to cooperate with your security plan, the employer still has a responsibility to protect the employee and co-workers on the premises. Under the General Duty Clause of the OSH Act, employers are required to take "feasible steps to minimize risks" in workplaces where "the risk of violence and significant personal injury are significant enough to be 'recognized hazards,'" according to a letter of interpretation provided by the Occupational Safety and Health Administration.

Some states allow companies whose employees have received

threats to obtain their own restraining orders to keep abusive part-
ners off the premises.

Before taking action against an employee suspected of being a
domestic violence victim, check state laws. Many states have laws
protecting the workplace rights of victims of domestic or sexual violence. Even in states that do not, employers should establish written
policies on leave requests and related issues. For model policies, see
the website of the Corporate Alliance to End Partner Violence.[9]

Q: Are employers allowed to have a policy forbidding guns in cars while at work?

In many states, the answer to this question is yes. An employer can
enforce a company policy or rule that requires employees to not
have guns in their cars while the cars are parked at work, even if the
employee has legally obtained a concealed-weapons permit.

However, some states restrict an employer's ability to enforce
a no-weapons policy in the workplace. Employers with employees
who work in these states are prohibited from restricting employees'
right to legally carry concealed weapons in their cars.

In any case, a best-practice approach is to train employees on
workplace violence prevention and have procedures for reporting
threats of workplace violence.

In addition, ASIS International and SHRM collaborated to
develop a *Workplace Violence Prevention and Intervention Standard*.[10] The standard provides an overview of policies, processes,
and protocols organizations can adopt to identify and prevent
threatening behavior and violence affecting the workplace, and to
better address and resolve threats and violence that have occurred.

Q: What should an employer do when one employee threatens another employee with bodily harm?

First conduct an investigation into the incident.[11] If the investigation reveals that the incident did occur, the next step is to document the incident and apply discipline in accordance with the severity of the threat and company policy or past practice. This could include separating the employees, counseling the offending employee about the impact of his or her behavior, providing a written warning, suspending the offending employee, or even terminating the employee. If the employee is not terminated, it may be appropriate to issue a final warning and continue to monitor the employee's behavior. If any further threats are made, immediate termination may be appropriate.

Employers should also take the following steps:

- Develop a written policy emphasizing that violence in the workplace will not be tolerated. The policy should clearly state what constitutes workplace violence and what constitutes acceptable and unacceptable behavior.
- Train all staff on workplace violence, and be clear on what steps to take if violence occurs.
- Establish a clearly communicated reporting system so that threats can be reported and investigated.
- Know the workforce. Assess threats and warning signs of workplace violence.
- Conduct a physical security and premises assessment.

The SHRM toolkit "Dealing with Violence in the Workplace" contains guidance on the implementation of workplace violence prevention programs.[12] In addition, ASIS International and SHRM have collaborated to develop a *Workplace Violence Prevention and Intervention Standard*.[13]

Q: How should an employer respond when an employee makes suicidal statements?

Suicide threats should always be taken seriously. The HR profes-

sional or the employee's supervisor may be the first person to identify a potentially suicidal employee, so it is critical to recognize the
warning signs and encourage at-risk employees to seek help.[14]

If an employee appears to be planning to take action immediately, local emergency authorities should be contacted because
employers are not usually qualified to handle such a situation
directly. If there are doubts as to whether the threat is immediate, the HR professional should contact local services, such as an
employee assistance program, suicide hotline, or hospital. Given the
risks of failing to take action, it is best to seek professional assistance as soon as possible.

If the threat becomes known through second-hand information,
it may be necessary to investigate the circumstances before taking
any action. Though unlikely, it is possible the comment was a casual
remark, made in poor taste, in reaction to excessive work-related
demands that may be addressed between the employee and the
supervisor. Assure the person who provided the information that the
employee's safety is more important than maintaining confidentiality. When it is not possible to obtain confirmation about the validity
of the threat, it is better to seek professional intervention through
one of the sources referenced in this section than to delay action.

Though it may be tempting, resist the urge to force the employee
to take time off or to require fitness-for-duty certification in response
to remarks involving suicide. Though the employee may have a condition that would fall under the coverage of the Americans with
Disabilities Act, employers should refrain from making such an
assumption.[15]

SHRM has compiled the following resources related to suicide
prevention:

- National Suicide Prevention Lifeline (http://www.suicidepre-
  ventionlifeline.org): 1-800-273-8255 (TALK). This is a
  national resource that may be accessed by anyone. If the

employee is a veteran, press "1" to access the Veterans Suicide Prevention Lifeline.

- Suicide Prevention Resource Center (http://www.sprc.org/).
- Working Minds: Suicide Prevention in the Workplace (http://www.workingminds.org/).
- American Foundation for Suicide Prevention (http://www.afsp.org/).

Appendix A
OSHA Forms for Recording Work-Related Injuries and Illnesses

OSHA
Forms for Recording
Work-Related Injuries and Illnesses

Dear Employer:

This booklet includes the forms needed for maintaining occupational injury and illness records for 2004. These new forms have changed in several important ways from the 2003 recordkeeping forms.

In the December 17, 2002 Federal Register (67 FR 77165-77170), OSHA announced its decision to add an occupational hearing loss column to OSHA's Form 300, Log of Work-Related Injuries and Illnesses. This forms package contains modified Forms 300 and 300A which incorporate the additional column M(5) Hearing Loss. Employers required to complete the injury and illness forms must begin to use these forms on January 1, 2004.

In response to public suggestions, OSHA also has made several changes to the forms package to make the recordkeeping materials clearer and easier to use:

- On Form 300, we've switched the positions of the day count columns. The days "away from work" column now comes before the days "on job transfer or restriction."
- We've clarified the formulas for calculating incidence rates.
- We've added new recording criteria for occupational hearing loss to the "Overview" section.
- On Form 300, we've made the column heading "Classify the Case" more prominent to make it clear that employers should mark only one selection among the four columns offered.

The Occupational Safety and Health Administration shares with you the goal of preventing injuries and illnesses in our nation's workplaces. Accurate injury and illness records will help us achieve that goal.

Occupational Safety and Health Administration
U.S. Department of Labor

What's Inside...

In this package, you'll find everything you need to complete OSHA *Log* and the *Summary of Work-Related Injuries and Illnesses* for the next several years. On the following pages, you'll find:

▶ **An Overview: Recording Work-Related Injuries and Illnesses** — General instructions for filling out the forms in this package and definitions of terms you should use when you classify your cases as injuries or illnesses.

▶ **How to Fill Out the Log** — An example to guide you in filling out the *Log* properly.

▶ **Log of Work-Related Injuries and Illnesses** — Several pages of the *Log* (but you may make as many copies of the *Log* as you need.) Notice that the *Log* is separate from the *Summary*.

▶ **Summary of Work-Related Injuries and Illnesses** — Removable *Summary* pages for easy posting at the end of the year. Note that you post the *Summary* only, not the *Log*.

▶ **Worksheet to Help You Fill Out the Summary** — A worksheet for figuring the average number of employees who worked for your establishment and the total number of hours worked.

▶ **OSHA's 301: Injury and Illness Incident Report** — A copy of the OSHA 301 to provide details about the incident. You may make as many copies as you need or use an equivalent form.

Take a few minutes to review this package. If you have any questions, *visit us online at www.osha. gov* OR *call your local OSHA office.* We'll be happy to help you.

An Overview:
Recording Work-Related Injuries and Illnesses

The Occupational Safety and Health (OSH) Act of 1970 requires certain employers to prepare and maintain records of work-related injuries and illnesses. Use these definitions when you classify cases on the Log. OSHA's recordkeeping regulation (see 29 CFR Part 1904) provides more information about the definitions below.

The *Log of Work-Related Injuries and Illnesses* (Form 300) is used to classify work-related injuries and illnesses and to note the extent and severity of each case. When an incident occurs, use the *Log* to record specific details about what happened and how it happened. The *Summary* — a separate form (Form 300A) — shows the totals for the year in each category. At the end of the year, post the *Summary* in a visible location so that your employees are aware of the injuries and illnesses occurring in their workplace.

Employers must keep a *Log* for each establishment or site. If you have more than one establishment, you must keep a separate *Log* and *Summary* for each physical location that is expected to be in operation for one year or longer.

Note that your employers have the right to review your injury and illness records. For more information, see 29 Code of Federal Regulations Part 1904.35, *Employee Involvement.* Cases listed on the *Log of Work-Related Injuries and Illnesses* are not necessarily eligible for workers' compensation or other insurance benefits. Listing a case on the *Log* does not mean that the employer or worker was at fault or that an OSHA standard was violated.

When is an injury or illness considered work-related?

An injury or illness is considered work-related if an event or exposure in the work environment caused or contributed to the condition or significantly aggravated a preexisting condition. Work-relatedness is

presumed for injuries and illnesses resulting from events or exposures occurring in the workplace, unless an exception specifically applies. See 29 CFR Part 1904.5(b)(2) for the exceptions. The work environment includes the establishment and other locations where one or more employees are working or are present as a condition of their employment. See 29 CFR Part 1904.5(b)(1).

Which work-related injuries and illnesses should you record?

Record those work-related injuries and illnesses that result in:

▶ death,
▶ loss of consciousness,
▶ days away from work,
▶ restricted work activity or job transfer, or
▶ medical treatment beyond first aid.

You must also record work-related injuries and illnesses that are significant (as defined below) or meet any of the additional criteria listed below.

You must record any significant work-related injury or illness that is diagnosed by a physician or other licensed health care professional. You must record any work-related case involving cancer, chronic irreversible disease, a fractured or cracked bone, or a punctured eardrum. See 29 CFR 1904.7.

What are the additional criteria?

You must record the following conditions when they are work-related:

▶ any needlestick injury or cut from a sharp object that is contaminated with another person's blood or other potentially infectious material.
▶ any case requiring an employee to be medically removed under the requirements of an OSHA health standard.
▶ tuberculosis infection as evidenced by a positive skin test or diagnosis by a physician or other licensed health care professional after exposure to a known case of active tuberculosis.
▶ an employee's hearing test (audiogram) reveals 1) that the employee has experienced a Standard Threshold Shift (STS) in hearing in one or both ears (averaged at 2000, 3000, and 4000 Hz) and 2) the employee's total hearing level is 25 decibels (dB) or more above audiometric zero (also averaged at 2000, 3000, and 4000 Hz) in the same ear(s) as the STS.

What is medical treatment?

Medical treatment includes managing and caring for a patient for the purpose of combating disease or disorder. The following are not considered medical treatments and are NOT recordable:

▶ visits to a doctor or health care professional solely for observation or counseling;

What do you need to do?

1. Within 7 calendar days after you receive information about a case, decide if the case is recordable under the OSHA recordkeeping requirements.

2. Determine whether the incident is a new case or a recurrence of an existing one.

3. Establish whether the case was work-related.

4. If the case is recordable, decide which form you will fill out as the injury and illness incident report.

   You may use OSHA's *301: Injury and Illness Incident Report* or an equivalent form. Some state workers compensation, insurance, or other reports may be acceptable substitutes, as long as they provide the same information as the OSHA 301.

How to work with the Log

1. Identify the employee involved unless it is a privacy concern case as described below.

2. Identify when and where the case occurred.

3. Describe the case, as specifically as you can.

4. Classify the seriousness of the case by recording the **most serious outcome** associated with the case, with column G (Death) being the most serious and column J (Other recordable cases) being the least serious.

5. Identify whether the case is an injury or illness. If the case is an injury, check the injury category. If the case is an illness, check the appropriate illness category.

U.S. **Department of Labor**
Occupational Safety and Health Administration

- diagnostic procedures, including administering prescription medications that are used solely for diagnostic purposes; and
- any procedure that can be labeled first aid. (See below for more information about first aid.)

What is first aid?

If the incident required only the following types of treatment, consider it first aid. Do NOT record the case if it involves only:

- using non-prescription medications at non-prescription strength;
- administering tetanus immunizations;
- cleaning, flushing, or soaking wounds on the skin surface;
- using wound coverings, such as bandages, Band-Aids™, gauze pads, etc., or using SteriStrips™ or butterfly bandages.
- using hot or cold therapy;
- using any totally non-rigid means of support, such as elastic bandages, wraps, non-rigid back belts, etc.;
- using temporary immobilization devices while transporting an accident victim (splints, slings, neck collars, or back boards).
- drilling a fingernail or toenail to relieve pressure, or draining fluids from blisters;
- using eye patches;
- using simple irrigation or a cotton swab to remove foreign bodies not embedded in or adhered to the eye;
- using irrigation, tweezers, cotton swab or other simple means to remove splinters or foreign material from areas other than the eye;
- using finger guards;
- using massages;
- drinking fluids to relieve heat stress

How do you decide if the case involved restricted work?

Restricted work activity occurs when, as the result of a work-related injury or illness, an employer or health care professional keeps, or recommends keeping, an employee from doing the routine functions of his or her job or from working the full workday that the employee would have been scheduled to work before the injury or illness occurred.

How do you count the number of days of restricted work activity or the number of days away from work?

Count the number of calendar days the employee was on restricted work activity or was away from work as a result of the recordable injury or illness. Do not count the day on which the injury or illness occurred in this number. Begin counting days from the day after the incident occurs. If a single injury or illness involved both days away from work, and days of restricted work activity, enter the total number of days for each. You may stop counting days of restricted work activity or days away from work once the total of either or the combination of both reaches 180 days.

Under what circumstances should you NOT enter the employee's name on the OSHA Form 300?

You must consider the following types of injuries or illnesses to be privacy concern cases:

- an injury or illness to an intimate body part or to the reproductive system,
- an injury or illness resulting from a sexual assault,
- a mental illness,
- a case of HIV infection, hepatitis, or tuberculosis,
- a needlestick injury or cut from a sharp object that is contaminated with blood or other potentially infectious material (see 29 CFR Part 1904.8 for definition), and
- other illnesses, if the employee independently and voluntarily requests that his or her name not be entered on the log.

You must not enter the employee's name on the OSHA 300 Log for these cases. Instead, enter "privacy case" in the space normally used for the employee's name. You must keep a separate, confidential list of the case numbers and employee names for the establishment's privacy concern cases so that you can update the cases and provide information to the government if asked to do so.

If you have a reasonable basis to believe that information describing the privacy concern case may be personally identifiable even though the employee's name has been omitted, you may use discretion in describing the injury or illness on both the OSHA 300 and 301 forms. You must enter enough information to identify the cause of the incident and the general severity of the injury or illness, but you do not need to include details of an intimate or private nature.

What if the outcome changes after you record the case?

If the outcome or extent of an injury or illness changes after you have recorded the case, simply draw a line through the original entry or, if you wish, delete or white-out the original entry. Then write the new entry where it belongs. Remember, you need to record the case most serious outcome for each case.

Classifying injuries

An injury is any wound or damage to the body resulting from an event in the work environment.

Examples: Cut, puncture, laceration, abrasion, fracture, bruise, contusion, chipped tooth, amputation, insect bite, electrocution, or a thermal, chemical, electrical, or radiation burn. Sprain and strain injuries to muscles, joints, and connective tissues are classified as injuries when they result from a slip, trip, fall or other similar accidents.

Classifying Illnesses

Skin diseases or disorders

Skin diseases or disorders are illnesses involving the worker's skin that are caused by work exposure to chemicals, plants, or other substances.

Examples: Contact dermatitis, eczema, or rash caused by primary irritants and sensitizers or poisonous plants; oil acne; friction blisters; chrome ulcers; inflammation of the skin.

Respiratory conditions

Respiratory conditions are illnesses associated with breathing hazardous biological agents, chemicals, dust, gases, vapors, or fumes at work.

Examples: Silicosis, asbestosis, pneumonitis, pharyngitis, rhinitis or acute congestion; farmer's lung, beryllium disease, tuberculosis, occupational asthma, reactive airways dysfunction syndrome (RADS), chronic obstructive pulmonary disease (COPD), hypersensitivity pneumonitis, toxic inhalation injury, such as metal fume fever, chronic obstructive bronchitis, and other pneumoconioses.

Poisoning

Poisoning includes disorders evidenced by abnormal concentrations of toxic substances in blood, other tissues, other bodily fluids, or the breath that are caused by the ingestion or absorption of toxic substances into the body.

Examples: Poisoning by lead, mercury,

cadmium, arsenic, or other metals; poisoning by carbon monoxide, hydrogen sulfide, or other gases; poisoning by benzene, benzol, carbon tetrachloride, or other organic solvents; poisoning by insecticide sprays, such as parathion or lead arsenate; poisoning by other chemicals, such as formaldehyde.

Hearing Loss

Noise-induced hearing loss is defined for recordkeeping purposes as a change in hearing threshold relative to the baseline audiogram of an average of 10 dB or more in either ear at 2000, 3000 and 4000 hertz, and the employee's total hearing level is 25 decibels (dB) or more above audiometric zero (also averaged at 2000, 3000, and 4000 hertz) in the same ears).

All other illnesses

All other occupational illnesses.

Examples: Heatstroke, sunstroke, heat exhaustion, heat stress and other effects of environmental heat; freezing, frostbite, and other effects of exposure to low temperatures; decompression sickness; effects of ionizing radiation (isotopes, x-rays, radium); effects of nonionizing radiation (welding flash, ultra-violet rays, lasers); anthrax; bloodborne pathogenic diseases, such as AIDS, HIV, hepatitis B or hepatitis C; brucellosis; malignant or benign tumors; histoplasmosis; coccidioidomycosis.

When must you post the Summary?

You must post the *Summary* only — not the *Log* — by February 1 of the year following the year covered by the form and keep it posted until April 30 of that year.

How long must you keep the Log and Summary on file?

You must keep the *Log* and *Summary* for 5 years following the year to which they pertain.

Do you have to send these forms to OSHA at the end of the year?

No. You do not have to send the completed forms to OSHA unless specifically asked to do so.

How can we help you?

If you have a question about how to fill out the *Log*,

❑ **visit us online at www.osha.gov** or

❑ **call your local OSHA office.**

U.S. Department of Labor
Occupational Safety and Health Administration

U.S. Department of Labor
Occupational Safety and Health Administration

Calculating Injury and Illness Incidence Rates

What is an incidence rate?

An incidence rate is the number of recordable injuries and illnesses occurring among a given number of full-time workers (usually 100 full-time workers) over a given period of time (usually one year). To evaluate your firm's injury and illness experience over time or to compare your firm's experience with that of your industry as a whole, you need to compute your incidence rate. Because a specific number of workers and a specific period of time are involved, these rates can help you identify problems in your workplace and/or progress you may have made in preventing work-related injuries and illnesses.

How do you calculate an incidence rate?

You can compute an occupational injury and illness incidence rate for all recordable cases or for cases that involved days away from work for your firm quickly and easily. The formula requires that you follow instructions in paragraph (a) below for the total recordable cases or those in paragraph (b) for cases that involved days away from work, and for both rates the instructions in paragraph (c).

(a) *To find out the total number of recordable injuries and illnesses that occurred during the year,* count the number of line entries on your OSHA Form 300, or refer to the OSHA Form 300A and sum the entries for columns (G), (H), (I), and (J).

(b) *To find out the number of injuries and illnesses that involved days away from work,* count the number of line entries on your OSHA Form 300 that received a check mark in column (H), or refer to the entry for column

(H) on the OSHA Form 300A.

(c) *The number of hours all employees actually worked during the year.* Refer to OSHA Form 300A and optional worksheet to calculate this number.

You can compute the incidence rate for all recordable cases of injuries and illnesses using the following formula:

Total number of injuries and illnesses x 200,000 ÷ Number of hours worked by all employees = Total recordable case rate

(The 200,000 figure in the formula represents the number of hours 100 employees working 40 hours per week, 50 weeks per year would work, and provides the standard base for calculating incidence rates.)

You can compute the incidence rate for recordable cases involving days away from work, days of restricted work activity or job transfer (DART) using the following formula:

(Number of entries in column H + Number of entries in columns I) x 200,000 ÷ Number of hours worked by all employees = DART incidence rate

You can use the same formula to calculate incidence rates for other variables such as cases involving restricted work activity (column (I) on Form 300L), cases involving skin disorders (column (M-2) on Form 300A), etc. Just substitute the appropriate total for these cases, from Form 300A, into the formula in place of the total number of injuries and illnesses.

What can I compare my incidence rate to?

The Bureau of Labor Statistics (BLS) conducts a survey of occupational injuries and illnesses each year and publishes incidence rate data by various classifications (e.g., by industry, by employer size, etc.). You can obtain these published data at www.bls.gov/iif or by calling a BLS Regional Office.

Worksheet

Total number of injuries and illnesses [ ] X 200,000 ÷ Number of hours worked by all employees [ ] = Total recordable case rate [ ]

Number of entries in Column H + Column I [ ] X 200,000 ÷ Number of hours worked by all employees [ ] = DART incidence rate [ ]

How to Fill Out the Log

The *Log of Work-Related Injuries and Illnesses* is used to classify work-related injuries and illnesses and to note the extent and severity of each case. When an incident occurs, use the *Log* to record specific details about what happened and how it happened.

If your company has more than one establishment or site, you must keep separate records for each physical location that is expected to remain in operation for one year or longer.

We have given you several copies of the *Log* in this package. If you need more than we provided, you may photocopy and use as many as you need.

The *Summary* — a separate form — shows the work-related injury and illness totals for the year in each category. At the end of the year, count the number of incidents in each category and transfer the totals from the *Log* to the *Summary*. Then post the *Summary* in a visible location so that your employees are aware of the injuries and illnesses occurring in their workplace. **You don't post the Log. You post only the Summary at the end of the year.**

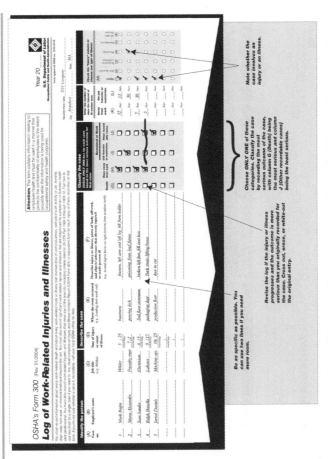

U.S. Department of Labor
Occupational Safety and Health Administration

OSHA's Form 300 (Rev. 01/2004)

Log of Work-Related Injuries and Illnesses

Attention: This form contains information relating to employee health and must be used in a manner that protects the confidentiality of employees to the extent possible while the information is being used for occupational safety and health purposes.

U.S. Department of Labor
Occupational Safety and Health Administration

Form approved OMB no. 1218-0176

Year 20 _____

You must record information about every work-related injury or illness that involves loss of consciousness, restricted work activity or job transfer, days away from work, or medical treatment beyond first aid. You must also record significant work-related injuries and illnesses that are diagnosed by a physician or licensed health care professional. You must also record work-related injuries and illnesses that meet any of the specific recording criteria listed in 29 CFR Part 1904.8 through 1904.12. Feel free to use two lines for a single case if you need to. You must complete an injury and illness Incident Report (OSHA Form 301) or equivalent form for each injury or illness recorded on this form. If you're not sure whether a case is recordable, call your local OSHA office for help.

Establishment name _____

City _____ State _____

Identify the person

Describe the case

Classify the case

CHECK ONLY ONE box for each case based on the most serious outcome for that case:

Remained at Work

Enter the number of days the injured or ill worker was:

Check the "Injury" column or choose one type of illness:

(A) Case no.	(B) Employee's name	(C) Job title (e.g., Welder)	(D) Date of injury or onset of illness	(E) Where the event occurred (e.g., Loading dock north end)	(F) Describe injury or illness, parts of body affected, and object/substance that directly injured or made person ill (e.g., Second degree burns on right forearm from acetylene torch)	(G) Death	(H) Days away from work	(I) Job transfer or restriction	(J) Other recordable cases	(K) Away from work	(L) On job transfer or restriction	(M) (1) Injury	(2) Skin disorder	(3) Respiratory condition	(4) Poisoning	(5) Hearing loss	(6) All other illnesses
			month/day			☐	☐	☐	☐	___ days	___ days	☐	☐	☐	☐	☐	☐
			month/day			☐	☐	☐	☐	___ days	___ days	☐	☐	☐	☐	☐	☐
			month/day			☐	☐	☐	☐	___ days	___ days	☐	☐	☐	☐	☐	☐
			month/day			☐	☐	☐	☐	___ days	___ days	☐	☐	☐	☐	☐	☐
			month/day			☐	☐	☐	☐	___ days	___ days	☐	☐	☐	☐	☐	☐
			month/day			☐	☐	☐	☐	___ days	___ days	☐	☐	☐	☐	☐	☐
			month/day			☐	☐	☐	☐	___ days	___ days	☐	☐	☐	☐	☐	☐
			month/day			☐	☐	☐	☐	___ days	___ days	☐	☐	☐	☐	☐	☐
			month/day			☐	☐	☐	☐	___ days	___ days	☐	☐	☐	☐	☐	☐
			month/day			☐	☐	☐	☐	___ days	___ days	☐	☐	☐	☐	☐	☐
			month/day			☐	☐	☐	☐	___ days	___ days	☐	☐	☐	☐	☐	☐
			month/day			☐	☐	☐	☐	___ days	___ days	☐	☐	☐	☐	☐	☐
			month/day			☐	☐	☐	☐	___ days	___ days	☐	☐	☐	☐	☐	☐

Page totals ▶

Be sure to transfer these totals to the Summary page (Form 300A) before you post it.

Public reporting burden for this collection of information is estimated to average 14 minutes per response, including time to review the instructions, search and gather the data needed, and complete and review the collection of information. Persons are not required to respond to the collection of information unless it displays a currently valid OMB control number. If you have any comments about these estimates or any other aspects of this data collection, contact: US Department of Labor, OSHA Office of Statistical Analysis, Room N-3644, 200 Constitution Avenue, NW, Washington, DC 20210. Do not send the completed forms to this office.

Page _____ of _____

OSHA's Form 300A (Rev. 01/2004)

Summary of Work-Related Injuries and Illnesses

Year 20____

U.S. Department of Labor
Occupational Safety and Health Administration

Form approved OMB no. 1218-0176

All establishments covered by Part 1904 must complete this Summary page, even if no work-related injuries or illnesses occurred during the year. Remember to review the Log to verify that the entries are complete and accurate before completing this summary.

Using the Log, count the individual entries you made for each category. Then write the totals below, making sure you've added the entries from every page of the Log. If you had no cases, write "0."

Employees, former employees, and their representatives have the right to review the OSHA Form 300 in its entirety. They also have limited access to the OSHA Form 301 or its equivalent. See 29 CFR Part 1904.35, in OSHA's recordkeeping rule, for further details on the access provisions for these forms.

Number of Cases

Total number of deaths

_____ (G)

Total number of cases with days away from work

_____ (H)

Total number of cases with job transfer or restriction

_____ (I)

Total number of other recordable cases

_____ (J)

Number of Days

Total number of days away from work

_____ (K)

Total number of days of job transfer or restriction

_____ (L)

Injury and Illness Types

Total number of . . .
(M)

(1) Injuries _____

(2) Skin disorders _____

(3) Respiratory conditions _____

(4) Poisonings _____

(5) Hearing loss _____

(6) All other illnesses _____

Establishment information

Your establishment name _____

Street _____

City _____ State _____ ZIP _____

Industry description (e.g., Manufacture of motor truck trailers) _____

Standard Industrial Classification (SIC), if known (e.g., 3715) _____

OR

North American Industrial Classification (NAICS), if known (e.g., 336212) _____

Employment information *(If you don't have these figures, see the Worksheet on the back of this page to estimate.)*

Annual average number of employees _____

Total hours worked by all employees last year _____

Sign here

Knowingly falsifying this document may result in a fine.

I certify that I have examined this document and that to the best of my knowledge the entries are true, accurate, and complete:

_____
Company executive   Title

(___) _____   ____/____/____
Phone   Date

Post this Summary page from February 1 to April 30 of the year following the year covered by the form.

Public reporting burden for this collection of information is estimated to average 58 minutes per response, including time to review the instructions, search and gather the data needed, and complete and review the collection of information. Persons are not required to respond to the collection of information unless it displays a currently valid OMB control number. If you have any comments about these estimates or any other aspects of this data collection, contact: US Department of Labor, OSHA, Office of Statistical Analysis, Room N-3644, 200 Constitution Avenue, NW, Washington, DC 20210. Do not send the completed forms to this office.

Optional

Worksheet to Help You Fill Out the Summary

At the end of the year, OSHA requires you to enter the average number of employees and the total hours worked by your employees on the summary. If you don't have these figures, you can use the information on this page to estimate the numbers you will need to enter on the Summary page at the end of the year.

How to figure the average number of employees who worked for your establishment during the year:

❶ Add the total number of employees your establishment paid in all pay periods during the year. Include all employees: full-time, part-time, temporary, seasonal, salaried, and hourly.

The number of employees paid in all pay periods = ❶ _____

❷ Count the number of pay periods your establishment had during the year. Be sure to include any pay periods when you had no employees.

The number of pay periods during the year = ❷ _____

❸ Divide the number of employees by the number of pay periods.

❶ _____ = ❸ _____
❷ _____

❹ Round the answer to the next highest whole number. Write the rounded number in the blank marked *Annual average number of employees.*

The number rounded = ❹ _____

For example, Acme Construction figured its average employment this way:

For pay period...	Acme paid this number of employees...	
1	10	
2	0	
3	15	
4	30	
5	40	
...	...	
24	20	
25	15	
26	+10	
	830	

Number of employees paid = 830 ❶

Number of pay periods = 26 ❷

830 = 31.92 ❸
26

31.92 rounds to 32 ❹

32 is the annual average number of employees

How to figure the total hours worked by all employees:

Include hours worked by salaried, hourly, part-time and seasonal workers, as well as hours worked by other workers subject to day to day supervision by your establishment (e.g., temporary help services workers).

Do not include vacation, sick leave, holidays, or any other non-work time, even if employees were paid for it. If your establishment keeps records of only the hours paid or if you have employees who are not paid by the hour, please estimate the hours that the employees actually worked.

If this number isn't available, you can use this optional worksheet to estimate it.

Optional Worksheet

Find the number of full-time employees in your establishment for the year. _____

Multiply by the number of work hours for a full-time employee in a year. X _____

This is the number of full-time hours worked. _____

Add the number of any overtime hours as well as the hours worked by other employees (part-time, temporary, seasonal) + _____

Round the answer to the next highest whole number. Write the rounded number in the blank marked *Total hours worked by all employees last year.* _____

OSHA's Form 301

Injury and Illness Incident Report

U.S. Department of Labor
Occupational Safety and Health Administration

Form approved OMB no. 1218-0176

Attention: This form contains information relating to employee health and must be used in a manner that protects the confidentiality of employees to the extent possible while the information is being used for occupational safety and health purposes.

This *Injury and Illness Incident Report* is one of the first forms you must fill out when a recordable work-related injury or illness has occurred. Together with the *Log of Work-Related Injuries and Illnesses* and the accompanying *Summary*, these forms help the employer and OSHA develop a picture of the extent and severity of work-related incidents.

Within 7 calendar days after you receive information that a recordable work-related injury or illness has occurred, you must fill out this form or an equivalent. Some state workers' compensation, insurance, or other reports may be acceptable substitutes. To be considered an equivalent form, any substitute must contain all the information asked for on this form.

According to Public Law 91-596 and 29 CFR 1904, OSHA's recordkeeping rule, you must keep this form on file for 5 years following the year to which it pertains.

If you need additional copies of this form, you may photocopy and use as many as you need.

Completed by _____

Title _____

Phone (____) ____ - ____   Date ___ / ___ / ___

Information about the employee

1) Full name _____

2) Street _____
   City _____ State ____ ZIP _____

3) Date of birth ___ / ___ / ___
4) Date hired ___ / ___ / ___
5) ☐ Male ☐ Female

Information about the physician or other health care professional

6) Name of physician or other health care professional _____

7) If treatment was given away from the worksite, where was it given?
   Facility _____
   Street _____
   City _____ State ____ ZIP _____

8) Was employee treated in an emergency room?
   ☐ Yes ☐ No

9) Was employee hospitalized overnight as an in-patient?
   ☐ Yes ☐ No

Information about the case

10) Case number from the Log _____ (Transfer the case number from the Log after you record the case.)

11) Date of injury or illness ___ / ___ / ___

12) Time employee began work _____ AM / PM

13) Time of event _____ AM / PM ☐ Check if time cannot be determined

14) **What was the employee doing just before the incident occurred?** Describe the activity, as well as the tools, equipment, or material the employee was using. Be specific. *Examples:* "climbing a ladder while carrying roofing materials"; "spraying chlorine from hand sprayer"; "daily computer key-entry."

15) **What happened?** Tell us how the injury occurred. *Examples:* "When ladder slipped on wet floor, worker fell 20 feet"; "Worker was sprayed with chlorine when gasket broke during replacement"; "Worker developed soreness in wrist over time."

16) **What was the injury or illness?** Tell us the part of the body that was affected and how it was affected; be more specific than "hurt," "pain," or "sore." *Examples:* "strained back"; "chemical burn, hand"; "carpal tunnel syndrome."

17) **What object or substance directly harmed the employee?** *Examples:* "concrete floor"; "chlorine"; "radial arm saw." *If this question does not apply to the incident, leave it blank.*

18) **If the employee died, when did death occur?** Date of death ___ / ___ / ___

Public reporting burden for this collection of information is estimated to average 22 minutes per response, including time for reviewing instructions, searching existing data sources, gathering and maintaining the data needed, and completing and reviewing the collection of information. Persons are not required to respond to the collection of information unless it displays a current valid OMB control number. If you have any comments about these estimates or any other aspects of this data collection, including suggestions for reducing this burden, contact: US Department of Labor, OSHA Office of Statistical Analysis, Room N-3644, 200 Constitution Avenue, NW, Washington, DC 20210. Do not send the completed forms to this office.

If You Need Help...

If you need help deciding whether a case is recordable, or if you have questions about the information in this package, feel free to contact us. We'll gladly answer any questions you have.

▼ Visit us online at www.osha.gov

▼ Call your OSHA Regional office and ask for the recordkeeping coordinator

or

▼ Call your State Plan office

Federal Jurisdiction

Region 1 - 617 / 565-9860
Connecticut; Massachusetts; Maine; New Hampshire; Rhode Island

Region 2 - 212 / 337-2378
New York; New Jersey

Region 3 - 215 / 861-4900
DC; Delaware; Pennsylvania; West Virginia

Region 4 - 404 / 562-2300
Alabama; Florida; Georgia; Mississippi

Region 5 - 312 / 353-2220
Illinois; Ohio; Wisconsin

Region 6 - 214 / 767-4731
Arkansas; Louisiana; Oklahoma; Texas

Region 7 - 816 / 426-5861
Kansas; Missouri; Nebraska

Region 8 - 303 / 844-1600
Colorado; Montana; North Dakota; South Dakota

Region 9 - 415 / 975-4310

Region 10 - 206 / 555-5930
Idaho

State Plan States

Alaska - 907 / 269-4957

Arizona - 602 / 542-5795

California - 415 / 703-5100

*Connecticut - 860 / 566-4380

Hawaii - 808 / 586-9100

Indiana - 317 / 232-2688

Iowa - 515 / 281-3661

Kentucky - 502 / 564-3070

Maryland - 410 / 527-4465

Michigan - 517 / 322-1848

Minnesota - 651 / 284-5050

Nevada - 702 / 486-9020

*New Jersey - 609 / 984-1389

New Mexico - 505 / 827-4230

*New York - 518 / 457-2574

North Carolina - 919 / 807-2875

Oregon - 503 / 378-3272

Puerto Rico - 787 / 754-2172

South Carolina - 803 / 734-9669

Tennessee - 615 / 741-2793

Utah - 801 / 530-6901

Vermont - 802 / 828-2765

Virginia - 804 / 786-6613

Virgin Islands - 340 / 772-1315

Washington - 360 / 902-5554

Wyoming - 307 / 777-7786

*Public Sector only

U.S. Department of Labor
Occupational Safety and Health Administration

Have questions?

If you need help in filling out the *Log* or *Summary*, or if you have questions about whether a case is recordable, contact us. We'll be happy to help you. You can:

▼ Visit us online at: **www.osha.gov**

▼ Call your regional or state plan office. *You'll find the phone number listed inside this cover.*

U.S. Department of Labor
Occupational Safety and Health Administration

Endnotes

Chapter 1

1. Occupational Safety & Health Administration, "OSH Act of 1970—Sec. 5. Duties," https://www.osha.gov/pls/oshaweb/owadisp.show_document?p_id=3359&p_table=OSHACT.

2. Occupational Safety & Health Administration, "Regulations (29 C.F.R. § 1910.151): Medical Services and First Aid," https://www.osha.gov/pls/oshaweb/owadisp.show_document?p_table=STANDARDS&p_id=9806.

3. Occupational Safety & Health Administration, https://www.osha.gov/.

4. Occupational Safety & Health Administration, "Standard Interpretations: 29 C.F.R. § 1910.151; § 1910.151(b)," December 11, 1996, https://www.osha.gov/pls/oshaweb/owadisp.show_document?p_table=INTERPRETATIONS&p_id=22314.

5. Occupational Safety & Health Administration, "Standard Interpretations: 29 C.F.R. § 1910.151," March 18, 1996, https://www.osha.gov/pls/oshaweb/owadisp.show_document?p_table=INTERPRETATIONS&p_id=22114.

6. Occupational Safety & Health Administration, "Standard Interpretations: 29 C.F.R. § 1910.151," July 2, 1991, https://www.osha.gov/pls/oshaweb/owadisp.show_document?p_table=INTERPRETATIONS&p_id=20323.

7. Occupational Safety & Health Administration, "OSHA Train-

ing: Courses, Materials, and Resources," https://www.osha.gov/dte/index.html.

8.   National Safety Council, Incident Investigation, 3rd edition, 2010, p. 7, http://www.nsc.org/news_resources/nsc_publications/Documents/soharDownloads/Incident_Investigation.pdf.

9.   Occupational Safety & Health Administration, "Standard Interpretations: 29 C.F.R. § 1910.1030, Most Frequently Asked Questions concerning the Bloodborne Pathogens Standard," https://www.osha.gov/pls/oshaweb/owadisp.show_document?p_table=INTERPRETATIONS&p_id=21010.

10. Society for Human Resource Management, "Health & Safety: Bloodborne Pathogens Policy," http://www.shrm.org/templatestools/samples/policies/pages/bloodbornepathogenspolicy.aspx.

11. Occupational Safety & Health Administration, "Standard Interpretations: 29 C.F.R. § 1910.1030, Bloodborne Pathogens," https://www.osha.gov/pls/oshaweb/owadisp.show_document?p_table=standards&p_id=10051.

12. Society for Human Resource Management, "Accidents and Injuries: What Are the Recommended Steps in an Accident Investigation?", September 6, 2012, http://www.shrm.org/TemplatesTools/hrqa/Pages/accidentinvestigation.aspx.

13. Occupational Safety & Health Administration, "OSHA Fact Sheet: Bloodborne Pathogen Exposure Incidents," OSHA Fact Sheet, January 2011, https://www.osha.gov/OshDoc/data_BloodborneFacts/bbfact04.pdf.

Chapter 2

1.   Society for Human Resource Management, "Have an Emergency Communications Plan," November 12, 2007, http://www.shrm.org/hrdisciplines/technology/Articles/Pages/CMS_006534.aspx.

2. Society for Human Resource Management, "Managing through Emergency and Disaster," March 25, 2013, http://www.shrm.org/TemplatesTools/Toolkits/Pages/ManagingEmergencyandDisaster.aspx.

3. Society for Human Resource Management, "Weather Conditions: Inclement Weather Policy," December 2009, http://www.shrm.org/TemplatesTools/Samples/Policies/Pages/CMS_000633.aspx.

Chapter 3

1. Society for Human Resource Management, "Americans with Disabilities Act of 1990 (ADA)," http://www.shrm.org/legal-issues/federalresources/federalstatutesregulationsandguidanc/pages/americanswithdisabilitiesactof1990(ada).aspx.

2. Occupational Safety & Health Administration, "OSH Act of 1970: Sec. 5. Duties," https://www.osha.gov/pls/oshaweb/owadisp.show_document?p_id=3359&p_table=OSHACT.

3. Society for Human Resource Management, "Americans with Disabilities Act of 1990 (ADA)," http://www.shrm.org/legal-issues/federalresources/federalstatutesregulationsandguidanc/pages/americanswithdisabilitiesactof1990(ada).aspx.

4. U.S. Department of Labor, "Fact Sheet #17G: Salary Basis Requirement and the Part 541 Exemptions Under the Fair Labor Standards Act (FLSA)," July 2008, http://www.dol.gov/whd/regs/compliance/fairpay/fs17g_salary.pdf.

5. Centers for Disease Control and Prevention, http://www.cdc.gov/.

6. Occupational Safety and Health Administration, https://www.osha.gov/.

7. World Health Organization, "Global Alert and Response (GAR): Pandemic (H1N1) 2009," August 10, 2010, http://www.who.int/csr/disease/swineflu/en/index.html.

8. Centers for Disease Control and Prevention, "Tuberculosis (TB)," last modified October 18, 2013,http://www.cdc.gov /tb/?404;http://www.cdc.gov:80/tb/faqs/default.htm.

9. Centers for Disease Control and Prevention, "Tuberculosis (TB): Fact Sheets," last modified April 12, 2012, http://www .cdc.gov/tb/publications/factsheets/default.htm.

10. Centers for Disease Control and Prevention, "Morbidity and Mortality Weekly Report (MMWR): Public Health Resources: State Health Departments," September 1, 2011, http://www .cdc.gov/mmwr/international/relres.html.

11. Occupational Safety & Health Administration, "OSH Act of 1970: Sec. 5. Duties," https://www.osha.gov/pls/oshaweb/owa-disp.show_document?p_id=3359&p_table=OSHACT.

12. Centers for Disease Control and Prevention, http://www.cdc .gov/.

13. Occupational Safety & Health Administration, "Seasonal Flu," https://www.osha.gov/dts/guidance/flu/influenza_a-vari-ant.html.

14. U.S. Equal Employment Opportunity Commission, "Disability Discrimination," http://www.eeoc.gov/laws/types/disabil-ity.cfm.

15. U.S. Equal Employment Opportunity Commission, "Summary: How to Comply with the Americans with Disabilities Act: A Guide for Restaurants and Other Food Service Employers," October 28, 2004, http://www.eeoc.gov/facts/restaurant _guide_summary.html.

16. Occupational Safety & Health Administration, "Toxic and Hazardous Substances: Bloodborne pathogens: 1910.1030," https://www.osha.gov/pls/oshaweb/owadisp.show_document ?p_table=STANDARDS&p_id=10051.

17. Occupational Safety & Health Administration, "Guidance on Preparing Workplaces for an Influenza Pandemic," 2009,

https://www.osha.gov/Publications/OSHA3327pandemic.pdf.

18. Centers for Disease Control and Prevention," Parasites - Lice - Head Lice: Frequently Asked Questions," http://www.cdc.gov /parasites/lice/head/gen_info/faqs.html#report.

Chapter 4

1. Society for Human Resource Management, "State Drug Testing Laws," June 2013, http://www.shrm.org/LegalIssues/State- andLocalResources/StateandLocalStatutesandRegulations /Documents/State%20Drug%20Testing%20Laws.pdf.

2. Society for Human Resource Management, "Employing Persons with Disabilities," May 22, 2012, http://www.shrm .org/TemplatesTools/Toolkits/Pages/EmployingPersonswith Disabilities.aspx.

3. Council of Better Business Bureaus, "FTC - Using Consumer Reports: What Employers Need to Know," June 29, 2010, http://www.bbb.org/council/migration/business-tips/2010/06/ ftc-using-consumer-reports-what-employers-need-to-know-/.

4. Federal Trade Commission, "Advisory Opinion to Islinger (06-09-98)," http://www.ftc.gov/policy/advisory-opinions/advisory-opinion-islinger-06-09-98.

5. U.S. Department of Transportation, "Am I Covered?" http: //www.dot.gov/odapc/am-i-covered.

6. U.S. Department of Transportation, "Office of Drug & Alcohol Policy & Compliance," November 5, 2013, http://www .dot.gov/odapc.

7. U.S. Department of Labor, "Drug-Free Workplace Act of 1988: Requirements for Organizations," http://www.dol.gov/ elaws/asp/drugfree/require.htm.

8. U.S. Department of Transportation, "Office of Drug & Alcohol Policy & Compliance," November 5, 2013, http://www .dot.gov/odapc.

9. Society for Human Resource Management, "State Drug Testing Laws," June 2013, http://www.shrm.org/LegalIssues/StateandLocalResources/StateandLocalStatutesandRegulations/Documents/State%20Drug%20Testing%20Laws.pdf.

10. Ibid.

11. Society for Human Resource Management, "Americans with Disabilities Act of 1990 (ADA)," http://www.shrm.org/legalissues/federalresources/federalstatutesregulationsandguidanc/pages/americanswithdisabilitiesactof1990(ada).aspx.

12. Society for Human Resource Management, "Health Insurance Portability and Accountability Act (HIPAA) of 1996," http://www.shrm.org/legalissues/federalresources/federalstatutesregulationsandguidanc/pages/healthinsuranceportabilityandaccountabilityact(hipaa)of1996.aspx.

13. Cornell University Law School, Legal Information Institute, "49 C.F.R. § 40.323—May Program Participants Release Drug or Alcohol Test Information in Connection with Legal Proceedings?" http://www.law.cornell.edu/cfr/text/49/40.323.

14. U.S. Department of Labor, "Drug-Free Workplace Policy Builder: Section 7: Drug Testing," http://www.dol.gov/elaws/asp/drugfree/drugs/screen92.asp.

Chapter 5

1. Cornell University Law School, Legal Information Institute, "Cardiac Arrest Survival Act of 2000," http://www.law.cornell.edu/topn/cardiac_arrest_survival_act_of_2000.

2. Division of Civilian Volunteer Medical Reserve Corps, https://www.medicalreservecorps.gov/HomePage.

3. National Conference of State Legislatures, "State Laws on Cardiac Arrest & Defibrillators," last modified January 2013, http://www.ncsl.org/research/health/laws-on-cardiac-arrest-and-defibrillators-aeds.aspx.

4. Occupational Safety & Health Administration, "General Environmental Controls: Sanitation: 1910.141," https://www.osha.gov/pls/oshaweb/owadisp.show_document?p_table=STANDARDS&p_id=9790.

5. Occupational Safety & Health Administration, "Regulations (29 C.F.R. § 1928.110): Field Sanitation," https://www.osha.gov/pls/oshaweb/owadisp.show_document?p_table=STANDARDS&p_id=10959.

6. Ibid.

Chapter 6

1. Occupational Safety and Health Administration, "Quick Reference Guide to the Bloodborne Pathogens Standard," https://www.osha.gov/SLTC/bloodbornepathogens/bloodborne_quickref.html.

2. Barbara D. Bovbjerg, "Federal and State Laws Restrict Use of SSNs, Yet Gaps Remain," General Accountability Office, September 15, 2005, ttp://www.gao.gov/assets/120/117096.pdf.

3. Occupational Safety & Health Administration, "OSH Act of 1970: Sec. 5. Duties," https://www.osha.gov/pls/oshaweb/owadisp.show_document?p_id=3359&p_table=OSHACT.

4. Society for Human Resource Management, "Workplace Monitoring Laws," http://www.shrm.org/legalissues/state-andlocalresources/stateandlocalstatutesandregulations/documents/state%20surveillance%20and%20monitoring%20laws.pdf.

5. Cornell University Law School, Legal Information Institute, "18 U.S.C Chapter 119—Wire and Electronic Communications Interception and Interception of Oral Communications," http://www.law.cornell.edu/uscode/text/18/part-I/chapter-119.

6.   Cornell University Law School, Legal Information Institute, "Omnibus Crime Control and Safe Streets Act of 1968," http://www.law.cornell.edu/topn/omnibus_crime_control _and_safe_streets_act_of_1968.

7.   Cornell University Law School, Legal Information Institute, "18 U.S.C. Chapter 119—Wire and Electronic Communications Interception and Interception of Oral Communications," http://www.law.cornell.edu/uscode/text/18/part-I/chapter-119.

8.   Society for Human Resource Management, "Workplace Monitoring Laws."

9.   Ibid.

Chapter 7

1.   Occupational Safety & Health Administration, "Most Frequently Cited Standards," https://www.osha.gov/dcsp/compliance_assistance/frequent_standards.html.

2.   Occupational Safety & Health Administration, "Standard Interpretations: 29 C.F.R. § 1910.1000," February 24, 2003, https://www.osha.gov/pls/oshaweb/owadisp.show_document?p_table=INTERPRETATIONS&p_id=24602.

3.   Susan S. Lang, "Study Links Warm Offices to Fewer Typing Errors and Higher Productivity," *Cornell Chronicle*, October 19, 2004, http://www.news.cornell.edu/stories/2004/10/warm-offices-linked-fewer-typing-errors-higher-productivity.

4.   Occupational Safety & Health Administration, "State Plans," https://www.osha.gov/dcsp/osp/.

5.   Occupational Safety & Health Administration, "Regulations (Standards—29 C.F.R.): Construction," https://www.osha.gov/pls/oshaweb/owasrch.search_form?p_doc_type=STANDARDS&p_toc_level=1&p_keyvalue=Construction.

6.   Occupational Safety & Health Administration, "Regulations (Standards—29 C.F.R.): Maritime," https://www.

osha.gov/pls/oshaweb/owasrch.search_form?p_doc_
type=STANDARDS&p_toc_level=1&p_keyvalue=Maritime.

7. Occupational Safety & Health Administration, "Regulations (Standards—29 C.F.R.): 1910," https://www. osha.gov/pls/oshaweb/owasrch.search_form?p_doc_ type=STANDARDS&p_toc_level=1&p_keyvalue=1910.

8. Occupational Safety & Health Administration, "OSH Act of 1970—Sec. 5. Duties," https://www.osha.gov/pls/oshaweb/ owadisp.show_document?p_id=3359&p_table=OSHACT.

9. Occupational Safety & Health Administration, "Regulations (Standards—29 C.F.R. § 1904.39): Reporting Fatality, Injury and Illness Information to the Government," https://www.osha.gov/pls/oshaweb/owadisp. show_document?p_table=standards&p_id=12783.

10. Occupational Safety & Health Administration, "Directory of States with Approved Occupational Safety and Health Plans," https://www.osha.gov/dcsp/osp/states_text.html.

11. Occupational Safety & Health Administration, "OSHA's Bloodborne Pathogens Standard," *OSHA Fact Sheet*, https:// www.osha.gov/OshDoc/data_BloodborneFacts/bbfact01.pdf.

12. Occupational Safety & Health Administration, "Regulations (Standards—29 C.F.R. § 1910.141): Sanitation," https://www.osha.gov/pls/oshaweb/owadisp.show_document ?p_table=STANDARDS&p_id=9790.

13. Occupational Safety & Health Administration, "Regulations (Standards—29 C.F.R. § 1928.110): Field Sanitation," https://www.osha.gov/pls/oshaweb/owadisp.show_document? p_table=STANDARDS&p_id=10959.

14. Occupational Safety & Health Administration, "Recordkeeping Forms and Recording Criteria: 1904.7," https:// www.osha.gov/pls/oshaweb/owadisp.show_document? p_table=STANDARDS&p_id=9638.

15. Occupational Safety & Health Administration, "Regulations (Standards—29 C.F.R. § 1904)," https://www.osha.gov/pls/oshaweb/owasrch.search_form?p_doc_type=STANDARDS&p_toc_level=1&p_keyvalue=1904.

16. Occupational Safety & Health Administration, "OSH Act of 1970," https://www.osha.gov/pls/oshaweb/owasrch.search_form?p_doc_type=oshact.

17. Occupational Safety & Health Administration, *OSHA's Field Operations Manual (FOM)*, November 9, 2009, https://www.osha.gov/OshDoc/Directive_pdf/CPL_02-00-148.pdf.

18. Occupational Safety & Health Administration, "OSHA Forms for Recording Work-Related Injuries and Illnesses," https://www.osha.gov/recordkeeping/new-osha300form1-1-04.pdf.

19. Ibid.

20. Occupational Safety & Health Administration, "OSHA Training: Courses, Materials, and Resources," https://www.osha.gov/dte/index.html.

21. For example, see AAA DUI Justice, "Sober Ride," http://dui-justicelink.aaa.com/for-the-public/aaas-role/public-education/sober-ride.

22. United States Census Bureau, "North American Industry Classification System," http://www.census.gov/eos/www/naics/.

23. *U.S. Equal Employment Opportunity Commission*, "Enforcement Guidance: Disability-Related Inquiries and Medical Examinations of Employees under the Americans with Disabilities Act (ADA)," July 27, 2000, http://www.eeoc.gov/policy/docs/guidance-inquiries.html.

24. U.S. General Printing Office, "49 C.F.R. Ch. III § 382.213, Controlled Substances Use." http://www.gpo.gov/fdsys/pkg/CFR-2010-title49-vol5/pdf/CFR-2010-title49-vol5-sec382-213.pdf.

25. Federal Aviation Administration, "Medications and Flying," http://www.faa.gov/pilots/safety/pilotsafetybrochures/media/

Meds_brochure.pdf.

26. Occupational Safety & Health Administration, "Ergonomics: Prevention of Musculoskeletal Disorders in the Workplace," https://www.osha.gov/SLTC/ergonomics/.

27. Centers for Diseases Control and Prevention, National Institute for Occupational Safety and Health (NIOSH), "Ergonomics and Musculoskeletal Disorders," last modified October 7, 2013, http://www.cdc.gov/niosh/topics/ergonomics/.

28. International Ergonomics Association, http://www.iea.cc/.

29. Human Factors and Ergonomics Society, http://www.hfes.org/web/AboutHFES/about.html.

30. ASTM International, http://www.astm.org/.

Chapter 8

1. Roy Maurer, "Company Data Endangered by Lack of BYOD Security," *SHRM Online*, August 17, 2012, http://www.shrm.org/hrdisciplines/safetysecurity/articles/pages/byod-security.aspx.

2. Society for Human Resource Management, "Technology: Laptop Security Policy," http://www.shrm.org/TemplatesTools/Samples/Policies/Pages/CMS_015063.aspx.

3. Dave Zielinski, "Bring Your Own Device," *HR Magazine*, February 1, 2012, http://www.shrm.org/Publications/hrmagazine/EditorialContent/2012/0212/Pages/0212tech.aspx.

4. Society for Human Resource Management, "Employee Relations—Legal & Regulatory Issues," http://www.shrm.org/LegalIssues/EmploymentLawAreas/EmployeeRelations%E2%80%94LegalRegulatoryIss/Pages/default.aspx.

Chapter 9

1. Centers for Disease Control and Prevention, *Costs of Intimate Partner Violence Against Women in the United States,*

March 2003, http://www.cdc.gov/violenceprevention/pdf/ipv book-a.pdf.

2. Occupational Safety & Health Administration, "OSH Act of 1970—Sec. 5. Duties," https://www.osha.gov/pls/oshaweb/owadisp.show_document?p_id=3359&p_table=OSHACT.

3. Occupational Safety & Health Administration, "Standard Interpretations - Table of Contents," December 10, 1992, https://www.osha.gov/pls/oshaweb/owadisp.show_document?p_table=INTERPRETATIONS&p_id=20951.

4. ASIS International and the Society for Human Resource Management, *Workplace Violence Prevention and Intervention Standard*, 2011, http://www.shrm.org/hrstandards/documents/wvpi%20std.pdf.

5. Society for Human Resource Management, "Domestic & Workplace Violence/Crime Victims/Weapons Laws," October 2013, http://www.shrm.org/LegalIssues/StateandLocalResources/StateandLocalStatutesandRegulations/Documents/Weaponsviolencelaws.pdf.

6. Occupational Safety & Health Administration, "OSH Act of 1970—Sec. 5. Duties."

7. Jennifer Camden-Chau, "When an Employee Obtains a Protection Order against Another Employee," *SHRM Legal Report*, September 22, 2009, http://www.shrm.org/LegalIssues/LegalReport/pages/protectionorder.aspx.

8. ASIS International and the Society for Human Resource Management, *Workplace Violence Prevention and Intervention Standard*.

9. Corporate Alliance to End Partner Violence, http://www.caepv.org.

10. ASIS International and the Society for Human Resource Management, *Workplace Violence Prevention and Intervention Standard*.

11. Society for Human Resource Management, "Investigations: How to Conduct an Investigation," April 22, 2013, http://www.shrm.org/TemplatesTools/HowtoGuides/Pages/How-toConductanInvestigation.aspx. See also Lisa Guerin, *The Essential Guide to Workplace Investigations: How to Handle Employee Complaints & Problems*, 3rd ed. (Berkeley, CA: Nolo/Alexandria, VA: SHRM, 2013).

12. Society for Human Resource Management, "Dealing with Violence in the Workplace," October 3, 2012, http://www.shrm.org/TemplatesTools/Toolkits/Pages/DealingWithViolen-ceintheWorkplace.aspx.

13. ASIS International and the Society for Human Resource Management, *Workplace Violence Prevention and Intervention Standard*, 2011.

14. National Institute of Mental Health, "Suicide: A Major, Preventable Mental Health Problem; Some Common Questions and Answers about Suicide," http://www.nimh.nih.gov/health/publications/suicide-a-major-preventable-mental-health-problem-fact-sheet/index.shtml.

15. U.S. Equal Employment Opportunity Commission, "Disability Discrimination," http://www.eeoc.gov/laws/types/disability.cfm.

Index

Additional
SHRM-Published Books

101 Sample Write Ups for Documenting Employee Performance Problems: A Guide to Progressive Discipline & Termination
Paul Falcone

The Essential Guide to Federal Employment Laws
Lisa Guerin and Amy DelPo

The Essential Guide to Workplace Investigations
Lisa Guerin

Healthy Employees, Healthy Business: Easy, Affordable Ways to Promote Workplace Wellness
Ilona Bray

HR at Your Service: Lessons from Benchmark Service Organizations
Gary P. Latham and Robert C. Ford

The Manager's Guide to HR: Hiring, Firing, Performance Evaluations, Documentation, Benefits, and Everything Else You Need to Know
Max Muller

SHRM Health Care Benchmarking
Society for Human Resource Management

Stop Bullying at Work: Strategies and Tools for HR and Legal Professionals
Teresa A. Daniel